THE OTHER
Russian Dolls

ANTIQUE BISQUE TO 1980s PLASTIC

Linda Holderbaum

SCHIFFER
PUBLISHING
4880 Lower Valley Road • Atglen, PA 19310

Other Schiffer Books on Related Subjects:

Dolls & Accessories 1910–1930s, Dian Zillner, ISBN 978-0-7643-2550-2

American Dollhouses and Furniture from the 20th Century, Dian Zillner, ISBN 978-0-88740-768-0

The Art of the Contemporary Doll, Sandra Korinchak, ISBN 978-0-7643-4860-0

Designed by Jack Chappell
Cover design by Brenda McCallum
Type set in Reforma/Argus/Minion

ISBN: 978-0-7643-5781-7
Printed in China

Published by Schiffer Publishing, Ltd.
4880 Lower Valley Road
Atglen, PA 19310
Phone: (610) 593-1777; Fax: (610) 593-2002
E-mail: Info@schifferbooks.com
Web: www.schifferbooks.com

For our complete selection of fine books on this and related subjects, please visit our website at www.schifferbooks.com. You may also write for a free catalog.

Schiffer Publishing's titles are available at special discounts for bulk purchases for sales promotions or premiums. Special editions, including personalized covers, corporate imprints, and excerpts, can be created in large quantities for special needs. For more information, contact the publisher.

We are always looking for people to write books on new and related subjects. If you have an idea for a book, please contact us at proposals@schifferbooks.com.

Contents

Acknowledgments 4

Introduction 5

1. Bisque: Antique 6

2. Bisque: To 1980s 26

3. Stockinette: 12 Inches and Taller 30

4. Stockinette: To 12 Inches 46

5. Composition 64

6. Plastic: 1960s Fifteen Republics 74

7. Plastic: Other 1960s–1980s, to 12 Inches 94

8. Plastic: Other 1960s–1980s, 12 Inches and Taller 110

9. Plastic Characters, Puppets, and Miscellaneous 130

10. Tea Cozies and Pincushions 148

11. Printed Reference Materials 162

Glossary of Clothing Terms 182

Russian Terms 189

Bibliography 190

Index 191

Acknowledgments

Without the encouragement of my father and mother, Jack and Betty Poirier, to explore the field of doll collecting, this interest, which grew over the years into a very rewarding and interesting hobby, would not have happened. And with it, the family trip to Montreal, Canada, to Expo '67 opened my eyes to the fascinating dolls of the entire world.

Sister, best friend, and fellow collector Rosemary Deal has continued to be my cheerleader and sounding board throughout this project. What fun we have had just getting our dolls together for the photo sessions!

The two people who have put up with the tables and counters full of dolls and resource materials as writing and photography were taking place deserve a hug and thank-you. My husband, Bob Holderbaum, has shown his patience as always while putting up with a sea of dolls. Son Josh Holderbaum has provided the patience and understanding of a collector, plus his help with editing, providing suggestions, and being a great technical supporter. Without their help this project would not have reached completion.

4

Introduction

Dolls are a mirror of man. They provide insight into other cultures and their people. They can teach us about their customs and social status and are miniature versions of the people themselves.

Since the 1960s, ethnic dolls, and Russian dolls in particular, have been a great interest of mine. Becoming frustrated with the lack of information available for these dolls or in some cases the misinformation that *was* available, I began accumulating what resource material I could gather for my own reference—the material that would eventually lead to this book.

Here we will explore dolls manufactured in Russia between the early 1920s and the 1990s and dressed in Russian clothing representing an ethnic group or historical costume. Dolls termed as "Russian," "peasant," or "village" are meant to depict representatives from the general Russian population and are outfitted in clothing worn in many areas. Specific regions or cultural groups are noted when possible; otherwise, no specific area can be pinpointed.

Dolls are arranged in order by date manufactured in most cases, beginning with the earliest dolls, the antique bisque and stockinette dolls, and followed by newer dolls as you move through the chapters.

I use "Russia" as a general term in this book. Dolls marked "MADE IN RUSSIA" were manufactured before 1922. The USSR (Union of Soviet Socialist Republics) was officially created in 1922 and dissolved in 1991. Borders of some of the countries included within the USSR have shifted periodically over time, leading to some difficulties identifying national costumes for some exact countries. And ethnic groups do not exist only within the boundaries of a particular country. Some of the cultures you will find here live in more than one country.

There are many Russian plastic dolls available from the same time periods; these are "play" dolls and are clothed in everyday clothing. Play dolls are defined as dolls produced and sold as playthings for children, as opposed to those sold as souvenirs or for display. Though made of the same materials, they are not included here.

Companies in other parts of the world have also produced dolls in Russian costume—some authentically costumed, some not. Those are not included in this book.

This is not a price guide. Prices these days are driven by what is popular at the moment, and vary so much from year to year that it is pointless to try to determine values.

Chapter 1
Bisque: Antique

When I began collecting dolls, I wanted to know everything about each doll I found—the maker, the year the doll was made, the material used, etc. I have since discovered that some of the most interesting dolls are those that have "sketchy at best" backgrounds and provide a continuing challenge to find their histories. The antique Russian bisque dolls produced during the 1920s and 1930s fall into this group. The early 1900s was a time period when the world was opening up—people were beginning to travel to exotic countries and wanted to bring back souvenirs and mementos for loved ones. Dolls representing many different countries began to be produced. German companies, located in the toy-producing center of the world, were the main producers.

There are some characteristics that are shared among these dolls. The height of the dolls falls between 10 and 16 inches. All have socket heads on composition and wood ball-jointed bodies that vary in production quality. The bodies are jointed at the neck, shoulders, elbows, wrists, hips, and knees.

While the heads are termed "bisque," most of them are actually terra-cotta, a ceramic material that is much more porous than bisque and fired at a lower temperature. The heads have a painted finish that looks dark and gives the dolls a deep, almost suntanned complexion—probably the interaction of the glaze with the terra-cotta material. The general consensus is that the heads were produced from Kammer & Reinhardt or Simon & Halbig molds. Very faint letters or numbers can sometimes be seen on the backs of the heads, but they are in most cases illegible if visible at all. Occasionally finer-quality bisques are found, created by German manufacturers then sold to Russian companies and dressed in Russian outfits. These outfits can sometimes be attributed to specific cultural or regional areas, but where noted as a "peasant" outfit they depict the typical Russian peasant dress seen throughout the country.

Every Road Together Is More Cheerful is the translated title from this Russian postcard printed in 1972, featuring two antique bisque dolls in original outfits.

attributed to cottage industries, where the work was done in homes by family members. Some of these made only doll heads, while others produced bodies and others did the costuming.

The most comprehensive information to date is from sources located by doll expert Elena Elagin that contain basic references to production centers. This includes a book by Galina Barto Dine titled *Sergiev Posad—the Capital of the Russian Toy* and an article by Boris Goldovskogo on "Danube" in his encyclopedia *Art Dolls*. Reference is made to a factory in Dunaeva, Hotkovo, that produced terra-cotta and porcelain objects. Hotkovo is a village in the area of Sergiev Posad (formerly called Zagorsk), the toy-producing center of Russia and one of the cities included in the Golden Ring, a ring of cities northeast of Moscow. These ancient towns are "open-air museums" and feature unique monuments of Russian architecture constructed from the twelfth to the eighteenth centuries. They are popular tourist attractions, and images of some of the buildings appear on nesting dolls. The factory was in operation from 1876 to 1937 and in 1908 employed about twenty people. By that time the plant was producing up to 15,000 pieces of terra-cotta, majolica, and porcelain. Models were copied from the German firm of Simon & Halbig. It was said their products received medals at exhibitions in Russia and abroad—with fourteen medals (five of them gold). In the early 1930s it included a brick factory as well. They stopped producing porcelain dolls in 1937, and the factory may have burned down during that time period. A house next to the factory caught fire and burned in 1980. These rather random details are the extent of our knowledge about the dolls' makers.

All have sleep eyes and open mouths with teeth. The eyes appear to be very flat on the surface, unlike the normal rounded glass eyes, and have a dull finish. While most of the dolls have pale-blue eyes, some brown eyes are also seen. The pale-colored eyes have a very small black pupil and black outline around the iris, which gives the dolls a staring or startled expression. Many of the eyes are too small for the eye sockets, with the colored iris not reaching to the edge of the sockets—also leading to a strange appearance. All have painted eyebrows and eyelashes. Most of the dolls have coarse flax-type hair that is blond, reddish blond, or red in color.

The majority of the dolls are dressed in peasant-type outfits seen in all regions of Russia and feature multiple layers of clothing. A few are dressed in outfits similar to those seen on some of the 15-inch stockinette dolls (see chapter 3). Almost all wear *lapti*, the basic peasant type of woven shoe. Basic clothing includes the *sarafan* or light sleeveless jumper. It is worn over a *rubakha* or blouse. This term is used for the blouses both of men and women. The embroidery along the neckline, sleeves, cuffs, and hem of the *rubakha* was believed to protect the wearer from evil. The most common color is white or red. The wraparound skirt or *poneva* was made of three straight, lengthwise strips of wool or linen. It was often made with a checkered pattern and decorated with ribbons and embroidery. It could open at the front or on the side or have no openings at all. Dolls dressed in fancier city-type outfits and elaborate historical outfits are much harder to find.

So where did these dolls come from? Exact company names and locations no longer exist. The dolls are often

Some of the dolls have small, 1-inch cloth labels with printed letters sewn to the outside of their clothing. Those marked "MADE IN SOVIET UNION" were produced after 1922; those with tags reading "MADE IN RUSSIA" were made before that date.

The ceramic material used for these socket heads is a terra-cotta-type, low-fire bisque. Made with a darker complexion, perhaps to depict the tanned peasant faces, here you see two of the terra-cotta heads compared with the fine bisque Russian lady below.

The glass eyes on many of the terra-cotta-headed dolls have a "buggy" stare with very pale eyes. I can only speculate that the eyes are a poor-quality material but may have been the only product available. This type of eye is smaller in size than those commonly found on most antique dolls, and the pupil is also very small. Between a very large pale-colored area of the eye and the small pupil, the eyes take on this "buggy" look.

Circa 1920 This elegant lady is 13 inches tall, 15 inches with her hat. Her head is constructed of good-quality bisque marked "132 / 0" and has blue sleep eyes and open mouth. Her ears are pierced but one hole does not go all the way through. She has a light-brown mohair wig in two braids. The head, made in Germany, was probably sold to a Russian company (either just the head or the head with body) and dressed in Russia.

She is on a ball-jointed composition body. The red fabric of her dress is probably representative of the traditional attire of the Saratov Province and is embroidered with a detailed design and turquoise, clear, and transparent-red seed beads are sewn on as accents. There are remains of red and white ribbon rosettes used as decoration on her stiff red hat. Yellow ribbon in delicate condition decorates her hat and her sleeves, as well as down the front of her bodice. She sports brown leather boots, and turquoise bead decoration can still be found on one boot.

There is no tag or label.

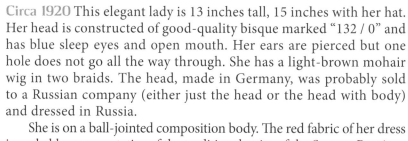

Prior to 1922 This pair of German bisque dolls was purchased together and seem to be a pair, even though the heads were made using different molds. They are dressed in typical peasant clothing. The boy is 15 inches tall and made by Armand Marseille. He is marked "1894 / AM 0 DEP / Made in Germany." He has an open mouth with teeth, coarse red hair, and wears pants, shirt, and coat with flannel hat. On the inside of his jacket he has a cloth tag that reads "No 1—22 / Made in Russia." Tied to his belt is a *rozhok* or flute. These wooden flutes can also be found on some of the large Russian stockinette dolls.

The girl has a similar tag on the front of her apron, but the printing has faded to white.

She is marked "Germany / C / 4/0." Her blond flax-type hair is gathered up in two buns high on the sides of her head, which are covered with a yellow kerchief that in turn is covered with the red scarf. Included with the various trim fabrics sewn to her sleeves are metal sequins at her upper arms and along the top edge of her apron. Both dolls wear identical woven *lapti* shoes and have the same type of leggings.

Circa 1920 These two delightful smaller German bisque dolls are harder to find, particularly in their original Russian outfits. It was popular in the early 1900s to purchase dolls in national costume as souvenirs when visiting a foreign country. These are dressed in unknown early provincial garb. Many were redressed when taken home and no longer have their original outfits. The taller girl is 6½ inches in height. She is an AM 1904, made by the German firm of Armand Marseille with a socket head on a composition body. She has an open/closed mouth with molded teeth and stationary blue glass eyes.

The shorter doll is 5 inches tall with a socket head on a composition body. She also has stationary eyes and an open mouth. Her costume is very elaborate and decorated with seed beads. Her very elaborate hat is decorated with seed beads, metallic lace, and sequins. Her closed vest is dark velvet and her clothing is sewn on. Both have painted shoes and socks.

Doll on right courtesy of Rosemary Deal

Circa 1920s–1930s This 3-inch (4 inch with the hat) German all-bisque doll is encased in a wonderful outfit with large *kokoshnik*. She has painted side-glancing eyes and painted gold feet and legs. She is jointed only at the shoulders. There is no tag, and we do not know if she was dressed in Russia or was just one of the many ethnic dolls in vogue at this time. While the region represented by this costume is unknown, many of the outfits have a very medieval look; a great many cultural outfits were patterned after thirteenth- and fourteenth-century clothing styles. Her clothing cannot be removed, and it is difficult to "peek" since the material is fragile.

You can see in the close-up photos the array of beads on her hat and the fine netting on her forehead, which also covers the back of her molded hair. Other variations of this doll have been seen with equally-as-elaborate costumes in various colors and decorated with a variety of beads, sequins, and lace.

Prior to 1922 This 15-inch doll wears a nineteenth-century outfit depicting a lady from the Ryazan area south of Moscow. Her head is a slightly finer terra-cotta than some of the other dolls. She has a vest over her *sarafan* and wears brown wooden and amber beads. Her hat has large white pom-poms and smaller blue ones. The white pom-poms on a lady's outfit would have been made of soft swan's down. You can see at her wrists there is elaborate crochet work. Her hat is tied at the back and has the coarse hemp-like twine on the back.

She has a cloth label sewn on to the front of her dress that reads "MADE IN RUSSIA," which dates her as being made before 1922. Tucked inside the front of this doll's *sarafan* we found a loose paper tag that reads "Avklädnings-Docka / Rättvik," which is Swedish for "undressed doll / Rättvik" (Rättvik is a municipality in Dalarna County, Sweden). Whether this tag is original to this doll or not is not known.

Courtesy of Rosemary Deal

Circa 1920 Standing 15 inches tall, this lovely lady is all original and in mint condition. Her costume is similar to those of the Saratov Province. She has an elaborate headdress with old metal sequins as decoration and a necklace of brown wooden beads. Her deeper-blue eyes give her a more normal look than most of the other dolls. The back of her headdress is tied at the top and has very coarse, woven, hemp-like twine around the back edge that hangs down as fringe. The bottom of her single braid has a red cloth strip braided into it. She has strips of fabric sewn on to her outfit, and a woven piece sewn to the bottom front edge of her dress. The woven piece is sewn on the sides and bottom but open at the top, like a pocket. She is marked with the number "35" on the back of her neck.

Courtesy of Rosemary Deal

11

Prior to 1922 These two lovely ladies wear identical outfits, though the dolls themselves are very different. Standing 10 and 11 inches in height, the taller one has a larger head that makes her look somewhat out of proportion when compared to the smaller girl. They both wear the *lapti* woven shoes and white pom-poms on their hats. While the region these dolls represent is unknown, the white pom-poms on their hats are similar to those worn by women of Mordwa.

Both dolls have dresses made of an off-white material with gold braiding sewn on, as well as the pale-blue beads, the same as seen in the necklaces that each doll wears. The "smaller-headed" doll has a cloth sewn on tag that reads "MADE IN RUSSIA" (dating her before 1922).

Doll on left courtesy of Rosemary Deal

Courtesy of Rosemary Deal

Prior to 1922 This 10-inch lady is in mint condition and wears an outfit similar to the Mordwa (a region of Russia also spelled Mordva or Mordvia) outfits seen on the large-sized Russian stockinette dolls later in this book. The coarsely woven linen outfit has a dropped waist, and there are triangular inserts under the arms of her dress. She wears amber beads and has four long, brown, wrapped braids, two in the front and two in the back.

Her pale eyes give her a staring expression. Her painted brows almost meet in the middle of her forehead. There is elaborate sewing on her hat, with four blue pom-poms on the top for decoration, and she has braids in the back. The front of her dress has a long geometric pattern down the front. The drop waist is belted just below her hips, and a piece of paisley fabric hangs from the belt. The same paisley fabric is repeated along the bottom edge.

Circa 1920s Rarely seen and difficult to find is this 14-inch beauty with an unidentified outfit. Her long, blond braids have ribbon woven into the hair, and the ends of both braids have interesting metallic ribbon tied in. Her unusual white felt-type or heavy flannel outfit has designs running down the front decorated with intricately modeled plastic buttons. The back of her costume is very plain. The fabric and trim on her hat matches her dress. She wears clear glass beads for her necklace. A cloth tag is sewn to the inside front of her dress, reading a faint "3 0." She is barefoot.

Circa 1920s This 14-inch doll is commonly referred to by collectors as a Gypsy and is very rare. Her outfit is similar to the outfits seen on the smaller stockinette dolls tagged Ziqanka, though the reference is unknown. She has a colorful red flowered-print dress with a patterned shawl tied under one shoulder. She has a very solid and heavy, brown, ball-jointed composition body that is a better quality than usual.

Her black braids have yellow ribbon as well as metallic sequins woven into them. The blue beads she wears may or may not be original. She has long, orange socks. The black shoes she wears are old and, again, may or may not be original to the doll.

The red-flowered material used on her dress is very similar to fabric seen on some of the other bisque dolls shown here. A round paper tag was found tied to her right wrist that reads "No. 1 - 56 - Made in Russia."

After 1922 Grouped here are two pairs of boy and girl dolls that were probably originally sold as pairs. All are 10 inches in height and in mint condition. One of the boys has a cloth tag that reads "MADE IN SOVIET UNION," dating them as being produced after 1922.

They have almost-identical coarse linen fabric for their tunics, with inset fabric yokes. One of the girls has the more unusual brown glass eyes as opposed to the blue glass eyes usually seen on these dolls.

The two boys have identical outfits, with different-patterned fabric on the inserts of their tunics. A coarse linen material is used for the shirts and the knee-length trousers, with different material used for the inset areas. Both wear the traditional *lapti* woven shoes and have wrappings around their lower legs. All wear unidentified costumes.

Pair of dolls on left courtesy of Rosemary Deal

14

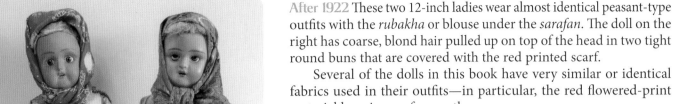

After 1922 These two 12-inch ladies wear almost identical peasant-type outfits with the *rubakha* or blouse under the *sarafan*. The doll on the right has coarse, blond hair pulled up on top of the head in two tight round buns that are covered with the red printed scarf.

Several of the dolls in this book have very similar or identical fabrics used in their outfits—in particular, the red flowered-print material here is very frequently seen.

In many European cultures and particularly in Russian tradition, the edging at the bottoms of the *sarafan*s was designed to protect the wearer from evil spirits.

The doll on the right has a paper wrist tag that reads only "USSR." You can also see the simple and somewhat crude modeling of her hands.

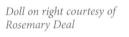

Doll on right courtesy of Rosemary Deal

Circa 1920s–1930s Standing 15 inches in height, this bisque is in pristine condition. She has a great deal of decoration on her apron and skirt, made of bands of embroidered cloth. She wears *lapti* shoes almost identical to the 15-inch German-made bisque pair seen earlier. Her blond hair, parted and styled into two buns on the top right and left on her head, is covered with the two head wraps. Threaded throughout the trim sewn to her sleeves are the tiny metallic sequins seen on several of the dolls. Her body is a good-quality composition, and her fingers are nicely molded with painted nails. She wears light-pink beads and has no tag or markings.

Circa 1920s–1930s This exotic lady stands 16 inches from her feet to the top of her hat. With sleeping blue eyes, her lips are painted in a style similar to the previous doll. She has a faint mark on the back of her head, but it is unreadable. The bisque under her hat is a darker, brighter orange color than the paler color on the rest of her face, indicating she must have been in intense light for a long period of time.

Her dress is a coarse-type material, and about 90 percent of the fabric is faded from sunlight exposure. A few areas on her outfit, such as the bright-pink ribbon that was used to decorate her blouse, have just a small amount still intact and still holding its color.

A woven wide strip decorates her apron. Rows of metallic braid trim and rickrack are used on the red skirt, with black-and-white plaid around the top part of the skirt. Her hat has floral designs made out of beads, though many are missing. The hat is lined on the inside and down the back with the same red paisley material that was used for the top inset on her sleeves.

After 1922 This cheery 11-inch couple have more "city-type" outfits typical of the urban Russians of the 1920s, though a specific area is unknown. The boy is bundled up for the cold with a thick flannel-type coat over a shirt and navy-blue knee-length pants. He wears the traditional *lapti* shoes and has reddish flax hair. He has a cloth tag that reads "MADE IN SOVIET UNION." His red-striped shirt has buttons on the side.

The lady wears a light-blue *sarafan* with a navy-blue shawl covering it. The shawl has interesting red plastic beads sewn along the edges. Her blond flax-type hair is braided and has been brought up to the sides of her head. The ribbons that hold the braids in place may be replacements.

Courtesy of Rosemary Deal

Circa 1920s–1930s This 11-inch lady is probably from Smolensk. She has trim on the front of her *sarafan*—it differs from the aprons seen on the large-sized Russian stockinette ladies from Smolensk because the trim goes all the way to the edge of the outfit. On the stockinette dolls it stops just before it reaches the bottom edge. Her pale-blue eyes have partly rolled up in her head; this is a problem that is common with these dolls—the weights that make the doll's eyes sleep are not correctly set. She is most likely missing a scarf that would have enclosed her headdress.

The back of her head has a small area where the bisque has pulled away, and in this area you can see the terra-cotta clay that she is made of. Her blond hair is bundled up under her hat.

Courtesy of Rosemary Deal

After 1922 This 11-inch lady is probably from the city due to her elaborate dark-green dress, though the specific area is unknown. She sports a paisley shawl to stay warm. The pink fabric that is used for the ruffles at her wrists is also used as the wrap for her blond hair.

Her cloth tag is found on the front under her shawl and reads "MADE IN SOVIET UNION."

The back of her outfit shows the two rows of ruffles that make her dress so elaborate. The ruffles, also of the same fabric as her dress, encircle the entire skirt.

Another doll wearing a similar dress was seen with a black hat with large flowers. We are not sure if this lady is missing the rest of her hat or the other lady just has a different hat.

Courtesy of Rosemary Deal

After 1922 This gentleman, 11 inches tall, has pale-blue sleep eyes in his bisque socket head with open mouth and teeth. His stiff gray hair represents an older man and gives him a somewhat unkempt appearance.

He could be depicting a well-to-do gentleman with his fancy printed coat (smoking jacket?). He has a printed shirt under a wine-colored jacket with blue pants. The over jacket is paisley fabric with extra-long sleeves. The garment is trimmed with yellow ribbon. He has a light-purple silk sash tied at his waist.

He wears a very strange hat on his head, with gray wool and a red-fabric top knot with a tassel. The gray color of the trim on his hat blends in with the gray color of his hair, making it difficult to distinguish where one stops and the other starts. He also sports red boots. He has no mark or tag but was probably made after 1922, and his region is unknown.

Circa 1920s–1930s Many layers of fabric cloth make up the generic peasant outfit on this 15-inch lady to keep her warm. She wears a *sarafan* and long flannel vest with lace trim at her sleeves. Her blond hair is tied up in braids that are wrapped around her head and tucked under her red printed scarf. Here you see some of the layers of clothing that she wears. The long vest is a flannel-type material with patterned cotton trim. The red flower-printed fabric seen under this vest is the same printed material seen on some of the other dolls in this book, and it must have been used in abundance.

Doll on right courtesy of Rosemary Deal

After 1922 Boys are less common to find among the bisque dolls. The largest boy is 15½ inches tall and the other is 14½ inches tall. Both wear the generic peasant blue knee-length pants, *lapti*, and wrapped lower legs, with traditional shirts plus navy flannel coats and hats. The taller boy has a slightly more elaborate decoration on the front of his white shirt. Here you can see the coarseness of his light-brown hair and bright-blue eyes.

The brown eyes of the smaller boy are very flat. He wears a red sash at his waist, while the taller boy wears a white sash. The smaller boy has a cloth rectangular tag sewn to the front of his jacket that reads "MADE IN SOVIET UNION."

Circa 1920s–1930s Wearing the same type and style of dress are these 15-inch dolls dressed in traditional peasant outfits worn throughout Russia. Their aprons are tied over printed blouses. Both have coarse strawberry blond hair with blue eyes and sweet features. One doll has suffered her hair being cut—we assume it would have been in a braid, like the other one.

Elaborate tatted lace is used on the sleeves and at the bottom of the apron on each doll. Both have two printed fabric underskirts beneath their *sarafan*s. The doll with the bobbed hair has a paper tag sewn to her apron that says "DOLL RUSSIA." She has a very faint star shape on the back of her head. The doll with the braid has the number "35" visible on the back of her head.

The cloth label sewn onto the apron of the doll reads "MADE IN RUSSIA."

Doll on left courtesy of Rosemary Deal

Circa 1920s–1930s These two ladies almost look like a mother and daughter. The taller doll is 15 inches, the smaller one 12 inches. Both wear the *rubakha* or blouse and skirt but also have aprons under their winter coats with fur trim.

The coats may be from the Voronezh Province or could be Ukrainian *suyta* (the right side of the coat is wider than the left in order to make a wedge-shaped overlay) and are a heavy dark-blue/gray flannel. The larger doll has elaborate crocheted trim on the edge of her apron. She has blond hair in two braids and wears what may be a replacement scarf.

The smaller doll's coat is dark gray with embroidered trim that goes down halfway on her right side and stops at the waist area. The trim on the coat on the larger doll goes all the way down the doll's right side from the neck line to the bottom edge of the coat. It looks like it would cover the other side of the coat, but there are no buttons to fasten the coat shut.

On the lower right edge of the coat's trim is a beaded design. These assorted glass beads are sewn on and are only in this spot. Other dolls with the same type of coat have also been seen with beads sewn in the same spot.

Courtesy of Rosemary Deal

Circa 1920s–1930s This pair has seen better days. Both dolls are 16 inches tall and wear the same flannel-style coat with red trim around the edge, depicting generic peasant garb seen throughout Russia. The coats are lined with printed material. The girl has a blouse, a skirt, and an apron with crocheted trim on the bottom. Her coat looks to be a tan color that has faded in the front. The boy's coat has a faint blue faded color on the back. Both have reddish-blond flax hair and wear *lapti* woven shoes.

The close-up of the girl's face shows a sad expression and dark complexion. Her eyes have probably been replaced or at least reglued. Glue has run down her cheek under her left eye and left a mark. The terra-cotta type heads cannot be cleaned easily. The boy has a few scuffs on his face. He has a shirt and blue patterned knee-length pants on under his coat. Tied to the front of his belt is a wooden comb similar to Imperial Russian wooden hand-carved combs from the early 1900s.

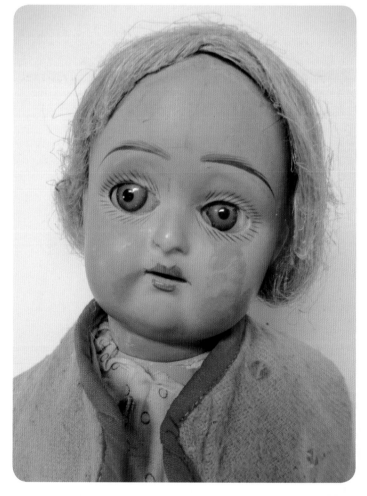

After 1922 These Ukrainian ladies have all original outfits. Both are 11 inches tall with pale-blue sleep eyes. Both wear dark scarves tied behind the neck, with fabric flowers on the top. Their white blouses have printed patterns that would have been embroidered on real outfits. Both dolls wear the typical red leather boot that is part of the traditional Ukrainian outfit, as opposed to the woven *lapti*.

The close-ups give you a better look at their headdresses, called *vinok*. Both dolls have brown hair that is barely visible, as opposed to the usual blond or reddish hair.

The doll with the red vest has a label on the front of her skirt that reads "MADE IN SOVIET UNION." The doll on the left has a blue vest with a red strip in her outfit. The patterns on her sleeves are different from the doll with the red vest.

The *kersetka* or sleeveless vest is fastened on the left with trim. They wear *plakhtas* or Ukrainian panel skirts woven in a square pattern.

Doll on left courtesy of Rosemary Deal

Circa 1920s This smiling peasant lady is 14 inches in height. The shoulder head appears to be made of a heavy ceramic material. Her features are painted on. She has a cloth body and individually sewn cloth fingers. She wears a *sarafan* and had a red skull cap (no hair) under her brighter pink kerchief. Her *sarafan* is faded turquoise—you can see the original deeper color in the folds and in areas on the back. A doll like this one was featured in the article "The Russian Doll" by Sandra F. Waugaman in the February 1993 issue of *Doll Reader Magazine*. In the article, the doll that was featured was given as a gift in 1923. These types of character dolls are not often seen. In addition to her *sarafan* or apron, she has underclothing as well as the traditional Russian shoes or *lapti*.

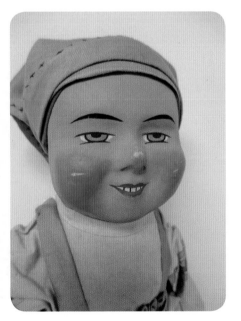
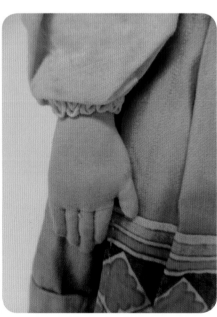

Circa 1930s This very unusual lady, 17 inches tall, has a shoulder head made of terra-cotta that has been undercoated in white and then painted. She has bisque painted hands that go up only to the wrist. Her cloth body is jointed at the hips so she can sit down. Her costume, its region unknown, is made of coarse linen. The multicolored patterns on her skirts are printed on. She has a very unusual hat. Remains of a paper tag were found attached to the back of her blouse, but no writing remains.

The original owner's father was a major general in the US Army serving as a military representative on the Allied Control Commission for Hungary. He purchased dolls abroad and sent them home to his daughter. The handwritten note with this doll said only "This doll is from Russia."

Chapter 2
Bisque: To 1980s

Modern bisque/porcelain dolls have been made from the 1970s to the present time and are readily available today. A gap in time has taken place due to the turmoil in the region caused by the various military conflicts as well as changes in manufacturing. During the 1950s and, as we will see, in the 1960s, plastic, a substance developed during the war years, became the material of choice in toys as well as in other areas. In the 1970s the hobby of doll collecting seemed to take off all over the world, and dolls of porcelain became very desirable; hence the reemergence of the porcelain doll for collectors and again as souvenirs. Since they are difficult to date, a sampling is included here to show you the types of dolls in this category.

The dolls can have a glazed porcelain shoulder head (very similar to the antique china head dolls, with the head and shoulders molded together and sewn onto a body) or can have an unglazed (matte finish) head, either as a shoulder head or a flange head (with the head stopping at the neck,

and with a rim around the edge so the head can be sewn onto the body). Features are painted on, hair is glued on, and they have porcelain hands and sometimes porcelain feet. They all have a pale or off-white complexion—the companies that made them did not attempt to give these dolls an authentic flesh-colored appearance. The dolls are not marked and are rarely tagged.

Clothing depicts the elaborate historical outfits from the seventeenth and eighteenth centuries, either copies of historical costumes or made-up versions. The costumes are decorated with a wide variety of trims, faux fur, and various types of beads.

Also popular with collectors are what I call "cone" dolls. They represent ladies in typical historical costumes and are constructed of white matte porcelain with porcelain hands. Their bodies are either porcelain or cardboard cones. There are no legs for these dolls. There are some male dolls that do have legs, but they are not jointed.

Circa 1980 These two 11-inch girls have bisque shoulder heads with perky faces and nice smiles with molded teeth. On cloth bodies, their bisque hands go up to the elbow. One has blond flax hair, and the other red. The girl with the scarf has her hair tied in a bun on the back of her head. They both wear long *rubakha* blouses with the stripe in the middle on the front and an apron. The blonde girl has a more elaborate outfit, with a flowered skirt underneath a red-and-ocher apron with rick-rack decoration. They both wear *lapti* shoes made of suede. The matte-finished porcelain heads have decaled eyes, pierced ears, and painted eyebrows and lashes. This type of matte-finished porcelain scuffs easily, so care needs to be taken with handling. From the same mold or series, they are not marked.

1980s to present Porcelain souvenir dolls such as these three ladies have been available since the 1980s and possibly before. Standing between 16 and 20 inches tall, they have porcelain heads, hands, and feet on cloth bodies. Similar to the cone dolls, they come in a variety of historical costumes. The girl in blue has a paper tag stating that her name is "Dasha" and that "she will remind you of Russia." The inside typed tag reads "My creator has dressed me in Russian 18th Century folk costume and head dress, made of velvet, silk and brocade, decorated with ribbons and beads to make it look pretty. My head, hands and feet are made from porcelain and fired at 1350 degrees C. They are very strong! My arms and legs are flexible and I can change position or sit on a chair."

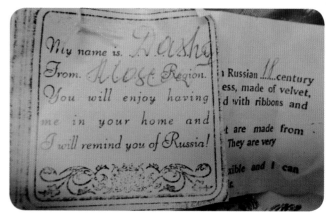

1970s to present Ranging in size from 4½-inch ornaments to 10½-inch ladies and men, these dolls with cone-shaped bodies have been produced from the 1970s to the present and are difficult to date for that very reason. They have white porcelain heads and hands with cloth arms. Their bodies are either porcelain cones or heavy cardboard cones. The ladies are dressed in various historical Russian outfits. A few men can be found dressed in regional clothing or military outfits, or representing a czar or historical figure. The clothing and ornaments are glued directly onto the dolls. Sometimes the cone bottoms are covered with cloth, with a stamp identifying the manufacturer, and sometimes they are just left open. They are carried by many Russian doll and toy distributors.

Circa 1980 This lady, 18 inches tall with her hat, has a porcelain shoulder head on a cloth body. Her bisque hands go just to the wrist. She has painted blue eyes and light-brown eyebrows, with an open mouth and molded teeth. Her hat is glued tightly to her head, and there is no hair.

There is no tag or mark. The matte bisque head has light scuffs to the finish that cannot be removed. With these dolls, care needs to be taken to avoid scratches to the porcelain.

Chapter 3
Stockinette: 12 Inches and Taller

During the past forty-five-plus years of doll collecting, some of the most intriguing Russian dolls encountered have been the cloth stockinette dolls, in particular the series of 14- to 15-inch dolls depicting adults. These were produced from the 1920s to the 1940s, and resource information has been hard to find and in some cases is less than accurate.

No information has been uncovered on who made the dolls. It is generally assumed that they were made in some type of cottage industry. With the uniformity of the face molds and painting of the facial features, as well as the consistency of costuming, perhaps they were distributed as kits and assembled by workers at home.

The doll heads are made of stockinette fabric over a form and depict adults. The bodies are constructed of cloth, with the stockinette used for the head and hands to the elbows. The fingers are molded together, with the thumbs held away from the fingers. The dolls are usually solidly stuffed and in a standing position. The facial features are painted onto the stockinette, with the eyes either looking straight ahead or

glancing to the side. Generally two or three face molds seem to be used. Eyebrows and nostril holes are also painted on. The cheeks are blushed. Either fading or an attempt at cleaning can be confirmed on faces with little color left. The faces vary depending on the culture of people being represented.

An aid in identifying the dolls can sometimes be found upon close examination of the undergarments. If you are fortunate you can find sewn somewhere onto the undergarments or inside of the skirt a white cloth tag with "MADE IN RUSSIA" or "MADE IN SOVIET UNION" printed on it, and in some cases the district and name of the doll. Dolls produced before 1922 are marked as Russian, and those produced after 1922 as Soviet Union. Some tags are printed in Russian instead of English. The cloth tags can also be found on the smaller stockinette dolls.

The dolls are made to represent various regions, cultural groups, or districts of Russia, which are now called oblasts. Districts that have been represented by the larger dolls include Smolensk, Nizhny Novgorod, Ukraine, Ryazan, and

Mordwa. Cultural groups include the Oroch, Eskimo, Samoyed, and a Village Boy. Additional regions mentioned in *World Color Dolls & Dress* by Susan Hedrick and Vilma Matchee include Belarus, Kursk, Orlovsky, and Voronezh, but dolls from these regions have not been verified. Where specific cultural or regional identification can be made, it is stated in each doll's description here. Otherwise the dolls are assumed to represent the typical Russian peasant.

One of the earliest sources of information on these dolls is a small photograph shown in *Notes on the Collection of Dolls and Figurines at the Wenham Museum* by Aledaine Cook, published by the Wenham (Massachusetts) Historical Association in 1951. The picture shows what is described as a complete set of thirteen of these dolls standing on a three-tiered shelf with a tea cozy doll on the bottom. Upon close examination of the photo, I have discovered there are at least three pairs of duplicate dolls shown on the shelves, so this contradicts the idea of a complete set. Dolls identified from the photo include one Ukrainian woman, two Smolensk, one Eskimo woman, two Mordwa, and two Ryazan. There are four unidentified dolls in the photograph; two of these, with large mittens and long coats, seem to be from the same region. In doing the research on these dolls, I have found, as in this example, that not all sources have accurate information.

Kimport Dolls, located in Independence, Missouri, offered for sale the Smolensk woman in the 1936 edition of their *Foreign Folk Dolls Catalog.* Selling for $3.00 each, the doll named "Tasha of Russia" represented the Smolensk district of Russia. She was described as "Face, hand painted of silk, is modeled with broad cheek bones, and strong but handsome features. Fabrics are typical, colorful and durable. Sabots are of woven fiber, legs bound with cloth stripping, because shoes and stockings are luxuries above their class." She is one of the more common dolls found in this size.

Village or "Willage" Boy

Circa 1920–1930 The other, probably most often-seen doll, is the "Village" or "Willage" Boy. And yes, the word on this boy's tags is spelled with a "W."

As with all ethnic-costumed dolls, the type of clothing we find on the dolls is tied closely to several factors: the geographic region of the people, the age of the person, the marital and economic status, the occasion the doll may be dressed for, and the accuracy of the manufacturer's depiction.

Smolensk Woman

One of the basic parts of the woman's outfit in the northern Russian area (typically around Moscow) is the *sarafan,* a light sleeveless jumper. It can be loose fitting or fitted at the waist and is worn over a *rubakha* or blouse. Prior to the Russian Revolution in 1917, the *sarafan* was made of red fabric, a color that symbolized beauty and was used in many Russian cultures for celebration costumes.

The wraparound skirt or *poneva* was worn in the southern and Slavic areas of Russia. It is made of three straight, lengthwise strips of wool or linen. It was often made with a checkered pattern and decorated with ribbons and embroidery. It could open at the front or on the side or have no openings at all.

The simple blouse or *rubakha* usually reaches to midthigh or full length. It can have full- or three-quarter-length sleeves. The embroidery along the neckline, sleeves, cuffs, and hem of the *rubakha* was believed to protect the wearer from evil. The most common color is white or red. This same term is used for the blouses both of men and women.

The man's shirt with the buttons offset at the collar is called a *kosovorotka.* The traditional shirt is long sleeved and reaches down to midthigh. There are buttons at the collar offset to the side, and the shirt is not buttoned all the way down. It is worn loose and not tucked into trousers but belted with a belt or ropelike tie.

Woven shoes are called *lapti* and are woven of bast, the bark of the linden or birch tree. The wood from this same tree is used to make the *matryoshka* or nesting dolls famous in Russia. All the dolls in this chapter wear the *lapti* shoes, with the exception of the Ukrainian dolls, the Oroch woman, and the Eskimo dolls.

There was a tradition in Russia that women always had to cover their hair. The belief was that the hair, especially that of a married woman, could attract evil spirits. Underneath the coverings, young women parted their hair in the middle and had a long braid in the back. Married Russian peasant women usually made two tresses and arranged them on the head or wore their hair in a bun. The headdress is evident in almost all the examples seen in this chapter except for a very few of the ladies that are representative of city dwellers who no longer follow the old cultural traditions.

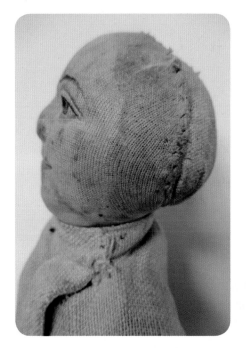 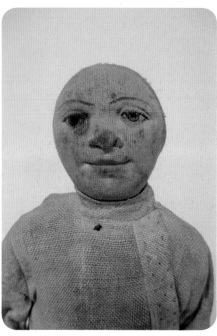 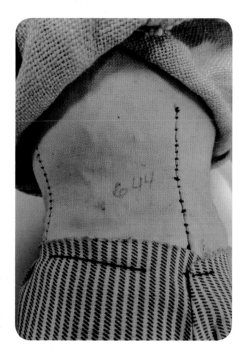

You can get an idea of the construction of these dolls by looking at this worse-for-wear Village Boy. The stockinette material used for his face does not cover his entire head but is sewn around the edges, much like a mask face.

The stockinette material on his arms goes up to the elbow area and stops. His body is a thick linen material and has a torso seam on his back.

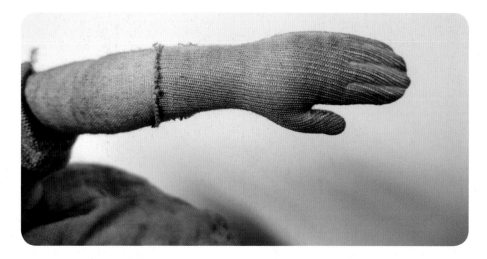

After 1922 Somewhere between the stockinette dolls and the tea cozies (see chapter 10) is this "attendant." Measuring 15 inches in height, this doll is in mint condition. She is constructed like the stockinette dolls but does not have legs. Her skirt is sewn together just above her knees, so she is not made like a tea cozy. There is a pocket in the front of her skirt—perhaps to store cooking utensils or to be used as a pot holder of some kind. She is dressed as a city lady and even wears fake pearl earrings. Her hair is fashioned into a bun on the back of her head. The fabric used on her underskirt is the same fabric that makes her collar.

Sewn on her underskirt is the printed label below: "MADE IN SOVIET / UNION / Attendant."

After 1922 The Eskimo, or *Esquimaux* in French, is a term for the indigenous people who have traditionally inhabited the northern circumpolar region from eastern Siberia (Russia) across Alaska, Canada, and Greenland. Samoyed was a term used in Russia for some of the indigenous peoples of Siberia. The Samoyedic peoples are those groups that speak the Samoyedic languages, which are part of the Uralic family. They are a linguistic group, not an ethnic or cultural one.

Pillow or cushion-like dolls can also be found representing them. They are without legs or feet, which gives them a sagging appearance. The doll with the white face is 12 inches and soft stuffed and has red, black, and dark green trim as well as white rabbit fur on the hem, wrists, and hood of her parka. There is no decoration on her back. The label sewn on the underside of this doll reads "MADE IN SOVIET UNION / Cushion Samoyed." This writing is barely discernible.

Slightly taller at 13 inches is the doll with the mink fur trim and darker face. She is soft stuffed and sagging. She has seen better days—her condition is poor, the white flannel material she is made of is worn, and the red felt trim sewn on for decoration has bled onto the adjoining fabric. The trim on her outfit—decorating just the front—is red, dark blue, and white. The white is difficult to see. She has mink fur trim on her outfit. There is no other discoloration on the parka fabric. She has side-glancing brown eyes, eyebrows, red nostril holes, and a red smile. There is no decoration on her back—she does not have any label or identification. She is stuffed with a very soft material like a cotton batting.

Doll to right courtesy of Rosemary Deal

After 1922 Eskimo dolls with legs also exist. These ladies, 14 inches tall, have cheery expressions. They both have tan bodies with white flannel pants. Their outfits have real rabbit fur trim and fabric designs of black, red, and green felt sewn on. They both wear mittens and boots. There are definite differences in condition between these two dolls—one in good shape, and one with peeling stockinette and missing fur.

Both have faces framed with light-brown rabbit fur. The back view of their outfits shows rows of brown rabbit fur trim and the three decorative cloth strips sewn on the back of the hood. One has strips of red cloth, and one has black strips. At the bottom of each strip are thin brass or tin circular pieces tied on. One hole is drilled into each of the circles. The boots are made of the same white fabric as their outfits and are stitched up the side with very little decoration. A thin red braid is sewn along the top edge of the foot on the front part of the boot. The cloth label, sewn into the inside of the parka on the doll in better condition, reads "MADE IN SOVIET UNION / Eskimo woman."

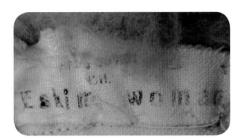
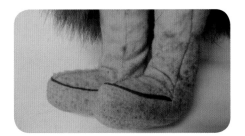

Doll on left courtesy of Rosemary Deal

After 1922 Here are two women representing the Mordwa District. Standing 14½ and 15 inches tall, they wear pants underneath their dropped-waist tunics, which have colorful fabric strips in pink, green, and blue. Printed designs representing embroidery can be seen at the neck, wrists, and hem of the tunics. *Lapti* are worn over wrapped leggings.

The head molds used for these dolls are different, with one having a broader and more serious expression. Their heads are wrapped with colorful ties in pink and blue, with no hair showing. One doll has white fur balls attached with clear beads to either side of her head, where the ears would be. Possibly these represent earrings.

Both dolls have fabric labels that read "MADE IN SOVIET UNION Mordwa Woman." One tag has blue ink, the other red ink. The Mordwa are one of the Finnish peoples who occupied parts of Russia. Cultural groups are not always contained within the borders of a specific country; another cultural group living in more than one country is the Lapp (Sámi) people.

The doll with the darker outfit has an elaborate necklace made of various beads that is sewn onto her bodice. Each doll has a square inset piece of fabric sewn into the armpit area. Each of the areas is outlined with what appears to be black paint.

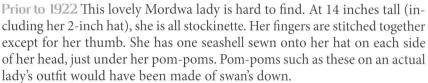

Prior to 1922 This lovely Mordwa lady is hard to find. At 14 inches tall (including her 2-inch hat), she is all stockinette. Her fingers are stitched together except for her thumb. She has one seashell sewn onto her hat on each side of her head, just under her pom-poms. Pom-poms such as these on an actual lady's outfit would have been made of swan's down.

There is braid trim along the front of her hat and also along the bottom edge. Her costume is red linen fabric and matches the material used for her hat. The beads are not original. She is missing her *lapti*. Her tag reads "MADE IN RUSSIA 4550 / Mordwa woman" (in blue ink).

Circa 1920–1930 Here are two examples of ladies from Nizhny Novgorod. Both are 15 inches tall and have good coloring with bright-pink cheeks and expressive eyes. Occasionally you find dolls in different poses, as seen with the doll with her hand up. It is actually sewn to her chin—there is no wire armature inside her body that bends the arm. Just a bit of hair shows under their scarves. The blouses have red thread stitched in a double row at the gathered wrists. The necks of the blouses are gathered, but there is no design or decoration and no design at the hem. The *sarafan*s have a gold patterned braid on the front and around the neck, with gold cloth "buttons." Their bottom edges are bordered by a wide band of paisley material. They are tied at the waist with a black-and-red ropelike belt. The dolls' outfits are topped off with a long vest trimmed in white fabric (one vest yellow and one orange). They wear leg wrappings and *lapti*. Their hats have gold trim sewn on in a geometric pattern, and black trim along the front above their foreheads. One doll has her cap covered with a black scarf with colored printed dots, the other with blue printed fabric.

The back view shows the gathering on the vests at the waist. The vests are lined with white fabric and have white trim. The doll with the orange vest has her cloth label, sewn on the front of her underskirt, printed in Russian in dark-blue ink that translates to Nizhny Novgorod, which is an oblast as well as the fifth-largest city in Russia and capital of that oblast. From 1932 to 1990 it was known as the Gorky Oblast.

Prior to 1922 This man, 15 inches tall, has a costume constructed the same way as the Mordwa women's, so he probably also represents the Mordwa region. His shirt has the inset sections seen in the dolls above on the underside/armpit of his shirt—here in red material, which matches the trim on his shirt.

He wears at his belt a wooden comb similar to Imperial Russian wooden hand-carved combs from the early 1900s. These combs can also be found occasionally on the Russian bisque dolls.

A square paper label is sewn to the bottom part of his shirt, with printing that reads "MADE IN RUSSIA," dating him as being made before 1922.

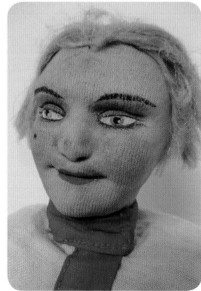

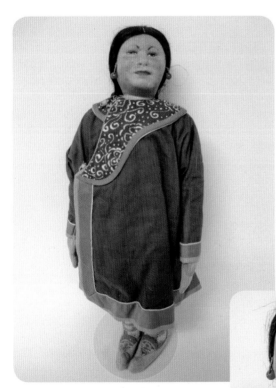

Circa 1920–1930 This 14-inch woman has a wonderful smiling face and brown eyes. Her Chinese-style dress opens at the side and is made of dark-gray cloth, with white paint making the decoration across the front. She wears red glass earrings and blue glass beads, the latter holding the garment closed. Her long, black hair is tied in two braids in the back, intertwined with red thread and glass beads.

She has very elaborate leggings that are painted with black and white designs. Her boots are painted with cutout designs that are glued on with slightly turned-up toes. Her label has unreadable blue printing in Russian on the top row, and handwriting in ink underneath that reads "Oroch woman."

The Oroch people live in Siberia. The Russian census of 2002 estimated those still speaking the Oroch language consisted of only approximately 250 people. Because they did not have written language, they were educated in the Russian language.

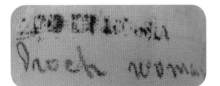

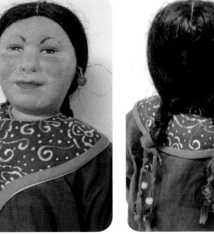

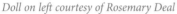
Doll on left courtesy of Rosemary Deal

After 1922 These Ryazan District women are most cheerful with their smiling faces. The open, smiling face is a different head mold than on most of the dolls. Again we see two different poses, with one woman's hand sewn at the waist. Standing 14½ inches tall, they have long, white *rubakha* with red-and-blue trim. Over this are dark plaid *poneva* or wraparound skirts that are gathered at the waist. Over that is a red-and-gray-on-white-patterned smock, which is open in the back. They wear *lapti* over their wrapped leggings. No hair is visible under their scarves. The blouses are gathered at the neck, with no decoration.

The back view shows that their aprons are open in the back and are not the traditional *sarafan*. The skirts are red, green, and black plaid with red fabric pieced into a front section. The label of the doll with the dark scarf is sewn on the front bottom of her *rubakha* in red ink and identifies her as being made before 1922: "MADE IN RUSSIA / Ryazan district woman" is on the right. The doll with the red scarf was made after 1922, since her tag reads: "MADE IN SOVIET / UNION / Ryasan district woman."

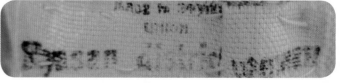

Doll on left courtesy of Rosemary Deal

Circa 1920–1930 These three 14½-inch ladies are from the Smolensk region, southwest of Moscow, and are the most commonly found of these large-sized dolls. The three also are good examples of the various conditions that these stockinette dolls can be found in. The basic outfit of the Smolensk woman consists of a blouse or *rubakha* in white linen with red embroidery on the sleeves, neck, and hem underneath the *sarafan*. All wear leggings, *lapti*, and scarves, either tied behind their head or wrapped around the neck and tied in the back. There are insets of red printed material on the shoulder areas of each doll.

The doll on the far left has an outfit that is slightly fancier, with more detail on her *sarafan* and with beaded earrings. She is in near mint condition. Her label, sewn onto her brown flannel underskirt, is printed in brown ink and reads "MADE IN RUSSIA / Smolensk district woman."

The doll in the middle has a pale complexion—it looks like someone tried to clean her face, which led to a loss of paint on her eyebrows and blush on her cheeks. The doll on the far right shows major condition problems. She is badly faded from prolonged exposure to sunlight, and the only remaining color to her *sarafan* is hidden in the folds, showing it was originally a bright-blue color. Her discoloration may also be due to having been exposed to cigarette smoke, kitchen fumes, or sunlight, which unfortunately is evident on other dolls seen in this book as well.

TASHA OF RUSSIA

SOME doll buys just naturally have more intrinsic value than others. We can't help it; we buy the best available offerings, from the strangest possible sources, and pass them on to you. This 15-inch woman from the Smolensk district in Russia, with her calm Slavic beauty and poise is an excellent value. Face, hand painted of silk, is modeled with broad cheek bones, and strong but handsome features. Fabrics are typical, colorful and durable. Sabots are of woven fiber, legs bound with cloth stripping, because shoes and stockings are luxuries above their class.

Supply Limited

No. 915—Smolensk Woman —$3.00

Also good buys are the boldly painted wood-carved figures done by peasants of Russian types.

No. 932—Russian Wood Figures. 9" _____95c

THE TEA SOAKER

Tasha of Russia, a 15-inch Smolensk Woman, was featured in an ad in the 1941 Kimport catalog for $3.00. Other Russian dolls also for sale included wooden figures as well as 6-inch stockinette dolls for 35 and 50 cents.

Circa 1920– 1930 This lady is pictured in the group photo of the dolls from the Wenham Museum but is not identified. Her right arm is bent up and actually sewn to her right cheek. Her left arm, also bent, is sewn to her right elbow. She has a smiling face, but not with teeth as do the other Ryazan ladies. The close-up of her apron shows the great detail and design on her apron, which is a full apron in the front. She has a skirt underneath, with dark material from side to back to side and a red strip sewn in the middle front, under her apron.

She has no identifying tag but is classified as another Ryazan lady because of her outfit design.

Circa 1920–1930 Here are two examples of Village Boys, probably the most common of the larger male dolls available. Though called a "boy," it definitely has an adult male appearance. Both have matching jackets and hats with wrapped leggings and *lapti*.

Both carry on a string a *rozhok* or flute in a conical tube shape. The *rozhok* traditionally has six playing holes: five on top and one underneath. The one here has six holes on top, but this shape matches this flute style more than any other type of Russian instrument. In the past these flutes were used by shepherds. Reddish-brown hair can be seen under their flannel-type hats. Both wear the shirt with the offset opening or *kosovorotka*. There is printed-on decoration to represent embroidery on the collar, sleeves, and bottom edges of the shirts. Both also have the cloth tag labeling them as "Willage Boy," with a "W" instead of a "V."

Circa 1920–1930 Here we have two very different Ukrainian ladies. The doll with the long ribbons and the long black vest is the more commonly seen of the Ukrainian dolls. This costume falls into the category of "*Vyshyvanka*," which has a general meaning that this outfit is composed of traditional clothing with embroidery. Her *rubakha* has printed-on embroidery along the sleeves and at the bottom hem. It is covered with a red-and-black-checkered skirt or *plakhta* that is split in the front. She also wears a black, long, sleeveless *kersetka* or vest that is midhip in length. Red and blue ribbons hang on the edge of her flowered *Vinok* headdress. She wears amber and turquoise glass beads and is not tagged.

The same face mold is used for both dolls, and both have their hair bare, depicting young or unmarried women. Each has their hair divided into two braids, which are tied up around the sides of the head.

The Ukrainian wreath or *Vinok* is a type of wreath that in traditional Ukrainian culture is worn by girls or young unmarried women. The wreath has symbolic meaning, and only specific flowers were used. The flowers were fresh, paper, or waxen and attached onto a band of stiff paper backing that is covered with ribbon. The *Vinok* is now worn by traditional Ukrainian dancers. Both wear the traditional red Ukrainian leather boots.

The lady with the shorter skirt and vest differs from the other dolls in several ways. One of the first differences seen is that she is jointed at the hips so she can sit. Also, the details on her outfit are not just printed on—embroidery on her blouse is actually sewn on. There are four real, white buttons sewn on the front of her blouse. She has a red-and-black-checkered velvet skirt—shorter than her counterparts—as well as a black velvet vest.

She appears to have the same face mold as the other Ukrainian doll and has side-glancing brown eyes. Her light-brown hair is carefully braided around the sides, with loops going to the top of her head. She has a red-and-black-checkered cap (the same material as her skirt) underneath her flowered *Vinok* headdress. Her cloth label, sewn to the front of her slip, is printed in blue ink, and, while written in Russian, it translates as "Ukraine."

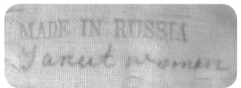

Prior to 1922 This Yakut Woman, 15 inches tall, is from the Siberian area of Russia and is extremely hard to find. Her outfit consists of two types of fabric pieced together—a red linen fabric on the sides and sleeves and a blue satin material down the front and as trim around the bottom of the outfit and at the bottom of the sleeves. The blue fabric has faded to a gray color from sunlight exposure. Some of the original blue color is visible around the bottom and on the back. She has the same red dangling decoration with thin tin circles sewn on to the ends, as seen on the Eskimo dolls. Fourteen round tin disks are also sewn to a tan piece of fabric attached to the front of her costume. The black fur trim on her outfit is mink. She wears black knee-high boots. Her cloth tag reads "MADE IN RUSSIA" and, in handwriting, "Yanut [or Yakut] woman." She has distinctly Asian features and is in extraordinary condition.

Circa 1920– 1930 Fresh from the garden is this 13½-inch lady. She has a friendly smile on her face, which is a longer, thinner face than on most dolls. She has blond hair with one braid in the back under her scarf. She wears a blouse with real embroidery instead of the printed-on patterns. Over this is a *sarafan* with red-patterned material and a yellow- and blue-striped border on the bottom. On top is a blue-and-white-printed apron. She holds in her right hand a stuffed and sewn fabric carrot. She is not tagged.

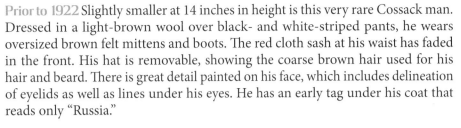

Prior to 1922 Slightly smaller at 14 inches in height is this very rare Cossack man. Dressed in a light-brown wool over black- and white-striped pants, he wears oversized brown felt mittens and boots. The red cloth sash at his waist has faded in the front. His hat is removable, showing the coarse brown hair used for his hair and beard. There is great detail painted on his face, which includes delineation of eyelids as well as lines under his eyes. He has an early tag under his coat that reads only "Russia."

Circa 1920–1930 Very stern looking and standing 15 inches tall in traditional Georgian clothing is this hard-to-find man. His jacket is brown unlined cotton. He wears knee-length black boots and flared black pants underneath. A tan long-sleeved shirt shows from under his jacket, with tiny black seed beads sewn on for buttons. Under the off-white turban he wears is a white felt hat with black trim. See chapter 6 for more information on this traditional costume.

The official national dress of Georgia included a full jacket for ease in getting into and out of the saddle. The front of his jacket has "patron pockets," which were originally used by Georgian men to store gun cartridges. The "bullets" are made of painted wood. This type of jacket was also worn by men from Armenia. He is not marked.

Circa 1920–1930 A matched pair, this rare 15-inch portly couple is most likely Ukrainian, and they have wonderful character faces. Both have embroidered designs on their clothing, done in matching thread. Each wears black boots. The lady wears a turban and has one earring missing. Her necklace consists of strands of green and red seed beads. She wears a dark velvet Ukrainian *kersetka* or sleeveless waistcoat over her knee-length blouse.

Her partner is a very jolly older man with an embroidered shirt and a traditional black *sharovary* (wide, baggy Ukrainian trousers), with a white sash at the waist. His wool hat is not removable. Tucked under his right arm is a white stuffed-flannel pig with open mouth, with separate stitched ears and black seed beads for eyes. Neither doll is marked.

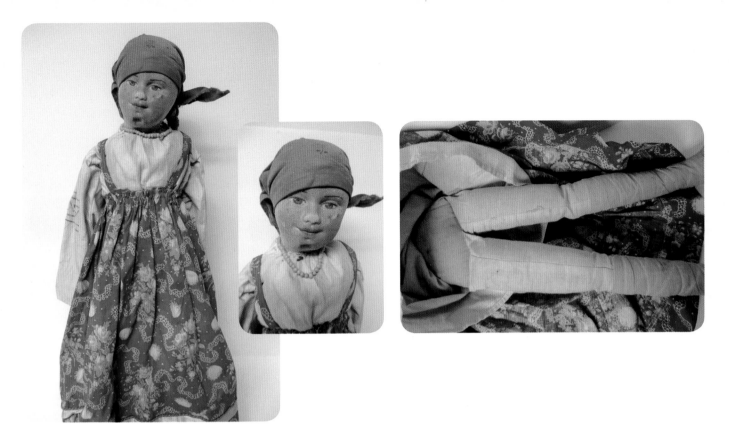

Circa 1920–1930 The peasant lady stands 23 inches tall. She has the same facial features as many of the tea cozies (see chapter 10). Under her skirt a small wad of stuffing was found, so she may have been a tea cozy converted to a doll. This conversion was most likely done long ago, since the material used for her body and legs appears old. She has two blond braids underneath her scarf. The design on the sleeves of her blouse is printed. A cloth tag exists under her skirt, but the printing is completely faded. Her face is slightly dented on the chin, and she has a nose rub, which is common for many of the dolls.

The large pair is also unusual. Standing 22½ inches tall, they are very solidly stuffed and heavy. They have sewn joints at the shoulders, elbows, hips, and knees so they can sit and be posed.

The faces, which use the same mold, are painted onto stockinette with the same style, and they both have stiff flax-type hair. The girl has embroidered designs on her *rubakha* or blouse, and the boy has printed designs on his silk *kosovorotka* or shirt. The boy's shirt has numerous small holes in the silk. Both wear identical *lapti*. They have no mark but appear to have been commercially made.

Chapter 4
Stockinette: To 12 Inches

More plentiful are the smaller stockinette dolls produced from the 1920s to the 1940s. In this chapter we will explore the dolls smaller than 12 inches. Most have stockinette or fine linen faces with painted features. Those that we would consider "pincushion" dolls can be found in a later chapter.

Most have painted features and simplified versions of the larger stockinette costumes. Some of these dolls were sold through Kimport Dolls in the late 1930s and 1940s, for $2.95 for 10-inch dolls down to 75 cents for smaller ones. The majority of these dolls are representative of the typical Russian peasant that was stereotyped from the 1930s into the 1950s.

In the descriptions I refer to "spoon" hands. This term is used to distinguish hands with fabric stretched over wire in a spoonlike appearance. The wire runs through the doll's torso in one piece, so if you move one arm, the other moves as well.

Look carefully for tags sewn on under an apron or underskirt or underclothes, sometimes high up (almost to the waistline). They wear smaller tags very similar to those found on the larger stockinette or bisque dolls, cloth and with printed words. Remember, if marked "MADE IN SOVIET UNION," they were produced after 1922. Dolls marked "MADE IN RUSSIA" were made before 1922.

Mordwa Women

This Kimport ad featuring three different small Russian stockinette dolls is from the 1944 catalog. The dolls representing peasant children were available for purchase for the low price of 35 cents to 50 cents.

After 1922 The 7½-inch dolls with the black-and-red outfits are Mordwa women. They are some of the more commonly seen small Russian dolls. They wear a red *tarboosh* hat. Their hands are mitten shaped out of stockinette, with a sculpted thumb as opposed to those dolls with the "spoon" hand. They wear white backpacks tied to their backs. The peasant boy and girl with a bundle also seen here are commonly found, as well.

Peasant Boy

Girl with a Bundle

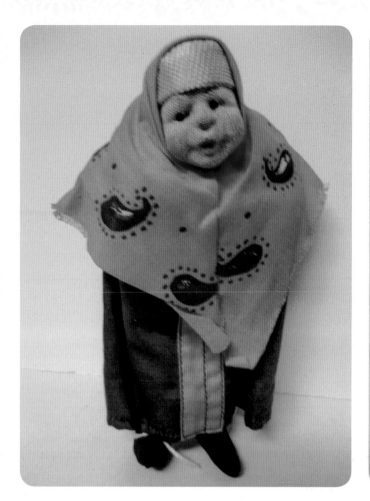
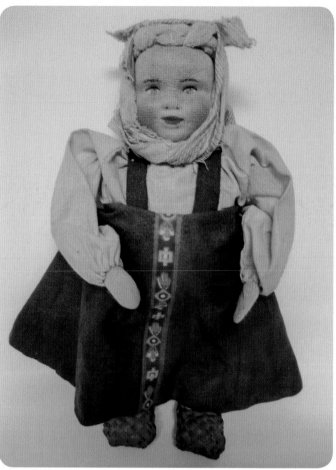

After 1922 These three girls are dressed in typical peasant costumes found throughout Russia. The faces have nicely sculpted features. The two 7-inch girls with the blue *sarafan* jumpers have the same face, with flax hair under their red-tinted scarves. The girl with the yellow strip down the front of her *sarafan* is marked "MADE IN SOVIET / UNION / C085 VELIKOVESSUN." They are among the more commonly found dolls in this size.

The slightly smaller 6½-inch girl has an unusual orange scarf decorated with a paisley pattern. She has an expressive face with side-glancing eyes and is harder to find.

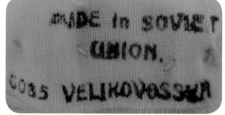

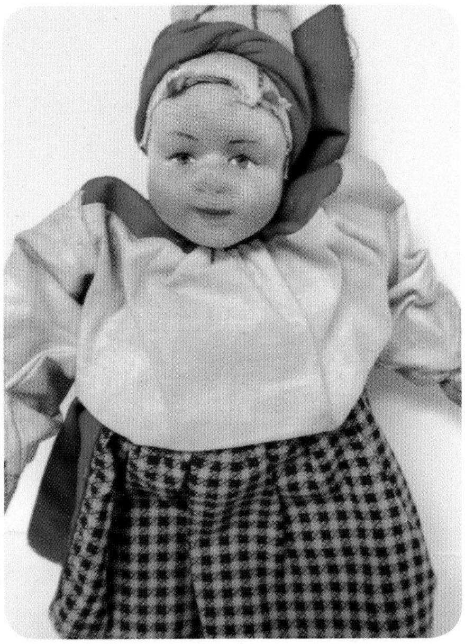

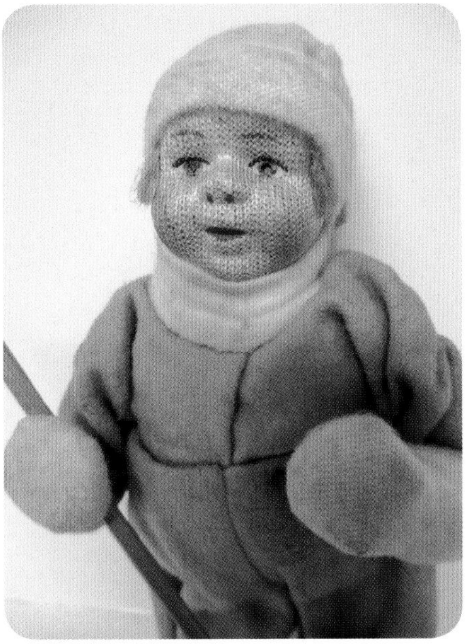

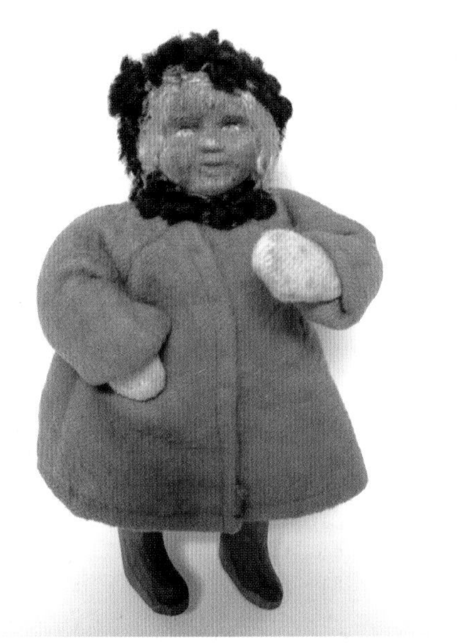

Her tag, which reads "MADE IN SOVIET / UNION / 8200 SKY-GIRL," probably should have read "SKI-GIRL."

After 1922 The checkered peasant skirt on the girl here has slits on both sides that show her white undergarments. She is 7 inches tall and has painted features and the typical spoon hands. Her hat is more unusual and is constructed of red and white material. She wears the traditional *lapti* shoes. Directly on her underwear is printed, in ink, "MADE IN SOVIET / UNION / [unreadable number/ letter] GIRL."

Harder to find is the 6-inch girl tagged "MADE IN SOVIET / UNION / 8200 SKY-GIRL," dressed in a flannel ski outfit as opposed to cultural dress. Probably she has lost her ski poles. Another harder-to-come-by doll is tagged "MADE IN SOVIET / UNION / 6064-A Winter Girl," dressed in the black faux fur hat and brown coat with wooden carved boots for her feet.

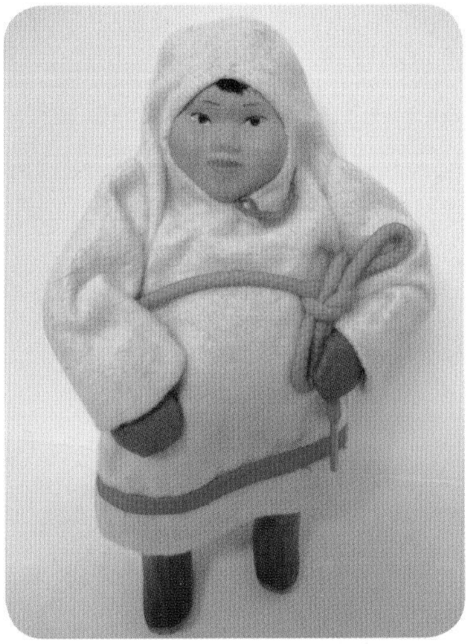

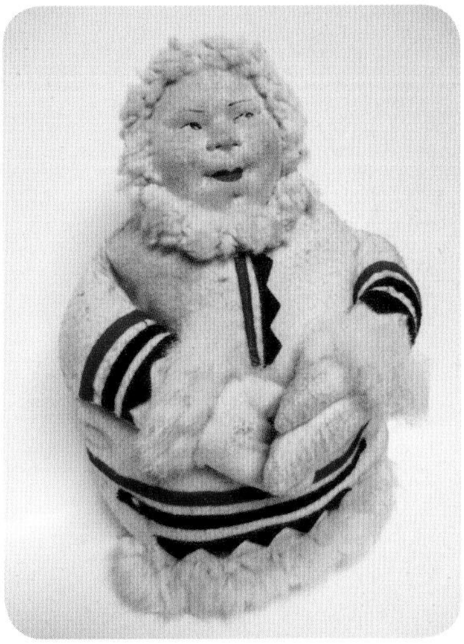

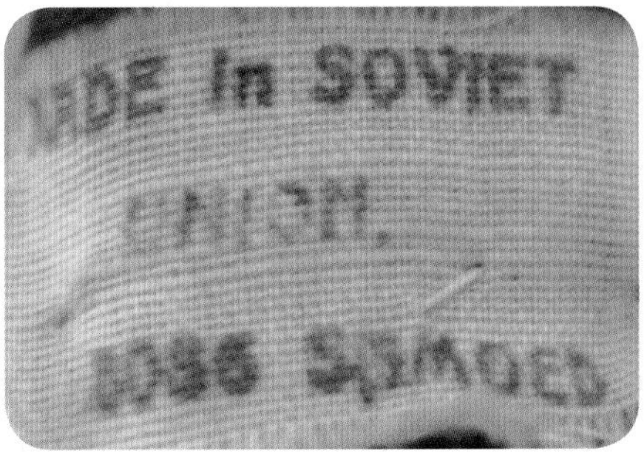

After 1922 This 7-inch doll has a white flannel outfit with brown cloth spoon hands and wire arms. The face is a darker stockinette fabric. It has carved wooden legs with boots. The outfit is very similar to that of the 12-inch pillow-type stockinette dolls marked "Samoyed." A red felt band decorates the lower edge of the outfit and is also used as a tie at the waist. The hood and the jacket are one piece of fabric.

"Samoyed" was a term used in Russia for some of the indigenous peoples of Siberia. The Samoyedic peoples are those groups that speak the Samoyedic languages, which are part of the Uralic family. They are a linguistic group, not an ethnic or cultural one. The cloth tag on the smaller doll has "Samoed" spelled differently, and, as we have seen, different or misspelled words do occur with these dolls.

After 1922 Another commonly found doll is this 7-inch boy with the large woven hat. His stockinette face has painted features, and he has the spoon hands with the wire arms that connect the two together. His olive-green sash is over dark-gray pants, and he has a red-yarn tie at the neck. He has wooden carved legs with boots painted black to go up to the knee.

A doll very similar to this is pictured in *European Costumed Doll Identification and Price Guide* by Polly and Pam Judd. The doll in the book is marked "MADE IN SOVIET UNION / Ziormra," but the exact region is unknown.

The boy with the black hat is an 8-inch boy from Tadjikistan. He wears a yellowish-colored turtleneck shirt and red- and yellow-striped pants. His lower legs are carved wood with the boots carved on—all painted black. His tag, found on the back under his coat, reads "MADE IN SOVIET / UNION / 8014 S. TADJIK." These boys can be found with various striped coats and several different types of hats made of faux fur.

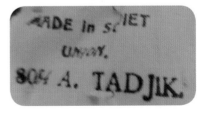

After 1922 A boy from Kirgiz, 7 inches tall, is shown with a 6½-inch girl from Uzbekistan. Both have wooden carved legs that include carved shoes with turned-up toes and the "spoon" cloth hands on wire frames. The boy has a red flannel coat belted low on his hips, with black-patterned cloth pants underneath and a white-flannel peaked hat with red machine-stitched trim. The Uzbek girls come in flannel dresses in plain colors or with printed patterns. A variety of headdresses, either as caps or with shallow pompoms, can be found on the girls. The boys traditionally wear the white felt hat.

The girl in the faded blue outfit is tagged "MADE IN SOVIET / UNION / UZBECHKA." The boy is tagged "MADE IN SOVIET / UNION / 8090 KIRQUIZ."

Courtesy of Rosemary Deal

The girl in the blue dress has this tag that identifies her as "MADE IN SOVIET UNION UZBECHKA."

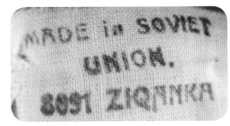

After 1922 Sometimes referred to as a "Gypsy," this 7-inch girl has a brightly designed gathered skirt over wooden carved legs and boots. She has the stockinette spoon hands and dark, curly hair under her scarf. The cloth tag sewn to her undergarments reads "MADE IN SOVIET / UNION / 8090 ZIQANKA." In doing research for this particular doll, I found that *ziqanka*, a type of Russian dance, is sometimes misspelled as *Ziganka*. The Gypsy population traveled throughout Europe, so this doll may be a representative of this population or an unknown regional group. Misspellings on tags or even within research material can lead to confusion in identifying these dolls.

The doll with the frown on his face is 6 inches in height and all original in typical peasant garb. A paper tag found with the doll but not attached (and there is no cloth tag) has typed on it the following: "RUSSIAN PEASANT / MAN ON THE ROAD / MADE IN USSR." The doll carries a wooden stick; hence the "on the road" part of the description. However, the doll does have a dress and is clothed as a female, so the "man" may have been a misprint.

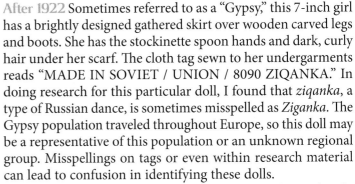

After 1922 Both of the girls with the light-colored generic peasant blouses are 6 inches tall, with printed cloth kerchiefs and smock blouses with machine-stitched edging. Both have the cloth spoon-type hands and wear *lapti*. The girl with the dark apron has a cloth tag sewn onto her undergarments that reads "MADE IN SOVIET / UNION / Mascha."

The girl in the darker outfit, from Byelorussia (today known as Belarus), is 6½ inches tall. She has blond mohair showing out from underneath her head wrap, and her hands are the spoon type wrapped in fabric. Her cloth tag, found up underneath her clothing, reads "MADE IN SOVIET / UNION / 6088 BELORUSSIA."

Circa 1920– 1930 Different in size and shape are these peasant dolls, all from the same series, with linen faces and painted features. They are all jointed at the hips so they can sit. The smaller dolls are 6 inches; the taller girl is 8 inches. The boys have elaborate hairdos made of light-colored soft yarn that is rolled up to make an "upswept" hairdo. The red-and-blue decorations on the boys' *kosovorotkas* are embroidered on instead of being printed on. The boy in the blue-trimmed shirt and the smaller girl have the same tag, which is sewn on to the back of their outfits. The tag translates as "Doll–[and a name]." The girls have simple peasant outfits, with the same type of hair under their scarves.

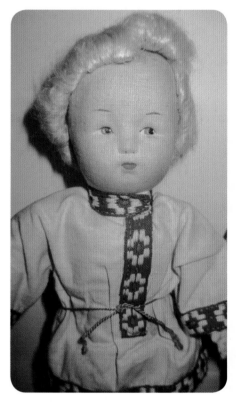

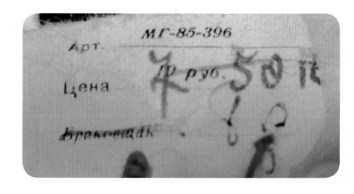

Circa 1920–1930 Two pairs of character couples, both with slightly different facial treatments, are shown here. All are 7½ inches with spoon hands. The pair with the man in the striped shirt and the lady with scarf have stockinette faces in worn condition. The faces, however, show great expressions, with side-glancing eyes and open mouths with smiles.

The couple that consists of the man in the dark hat and woman without a hat are equally as expressive. The heads on these two dolls are also cloth but appear to have been completely painted, not just the facial features. The woman has lost her head covering. All wear *lapti* and have spoon hands. There are no tags on either couple. Like many of the dolls in this chapter, they represent the generic Russian peasant that could be seen in all areas of Russia during this time period.

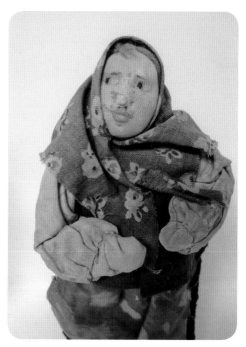

After 1922 Jointed at the shoulders and hips are these two identical dolls, both in their original boxes, though one is shown from the back, out of her box. The red fabric used on their headdresses is also used for the top of their outfits. Printed designs decorated their aprons. In pristine condition, they have a different type of identification. An ink handwritten tag is sewn to the undergarments of each doll, which reads "1855 MADE IN THE / SOVIET UNION." There is no identification on the boxes, which are an inexpensive, plain cardboard box with separate lid. They are more examples representing the generic Russian peasant.

After 1922 White-and-red cloth makes up the outfit (probably from Ryazan) on this 8-inch girl, who is jointed at the shoulders and hips. Her hands are cloth and formed as straight stubs with no defined "hands." The red trim on her outfit is sewn on with machine stitching. Her black cloth shoes are sewn on as well. There are pom-poms sewn on to the sides of her hat. There is also a pom-pom sewn onto the back of her head-dress. The white pom-poms on a lady's outfit would have been made of soft swan's down.

The same sweet face mold is used for the doll in peasant outfit with the red scarf, which also stands 8 inches tall. She is all original, with a patterned skirt underneath her white coat and red scarf. She has a cloth label on her underskirt that reads "860 MADE IN / SOVIET UNION."

Circa 1930–1940 Sporting a black wool cap is a 9-inch peasant boy with brown flax-type hair peeking out from under his hat. His spoon hands meet in the front. The left hand, sewn to his shirt, holds a piece of red floral-printed fabric. He wears *lapti* that are almost oversized for his body. He is identified as a doll sold through Kimport Dolls, since he has sewn under his shirt a square Kimport tag. Kimport-tagged dolls they sold with this tag and typed onto the tags denoted the countries the dolls represented. In this case, "Made in / Russia" is typed on.

Slightly taller at 11 inches tall is this boy dressed in a peasant's winter coat, with a completely painted stockinette face. It appears that only the front part of his face was painted. The back of the head is not stockinette, but unpainted cloth. He may have been repainted or this may be original to the doll. He wears his *lapti*, shirt, and pants, as well as a tan-colored wool felt coat complete with faux fur collar. His hat is felt and of a "sailor type" with a brim on the front. He has no tags. His coat could be an *armiak*—a heavy cloth coat worn mainly by men, with a right-to-left wrap-over that also had a large collar. In the eighteenth to early twentieth centuries the *armiak* was mainly a peasant's dress.

If you are a stickler for getting the correct terms for your doll's clothing, it can be confusing depending on the region you are researching, and terminology can become frustrating. As an example, there are at least twelve different Russian words for coat: *armiak, fereza, katanka, kholodnik, koshan, kurtka, okhaben, platno, privoloka, shuba, torlop,* and *tulup.*

Circa 1930–1940 Different from the dolls seen above are these character dolls with closed eyes and smiles.

Both couples, 10 inches in height, have lashes embroidered on. Sometimes names are printed on, such as Alexei or Tanika. Each boy wears a tag reading "MADE IN SOVIET / UNION / 203-VANIKA." Each girl here is marked "FOREIGN / Made / 8202 AKOULINA."

Shown here is a press photo dated on the back June 30, 1935. A handwritten description on the back reads

Two Russian Honeymoon dolls . . . from the Styll collection. This photo was cut and pasted with a photo of a single Basque boy doll. This photo was used as part of an article printed in the *Battle Creek Enquirer and Evening News* on Sunday, June 30, 1935. The article was titled "Looking into the Fascinating History of Dolls."

Circa 1930–1940 Olga, Anna, and Sonia, all in typical Russian peasant outfits, are pictured here. Their names are found in an ad featuring the three 10-inch girls in the 1944 issue of the *Foreign Folk Doll Catalog*, produced by Kimport Dolls from Independence, Missouri. Anna, seen in the middle of the Kimport ad, wears a dark vest and matching hat decorated with lace rosettes. She has a red skirt and white lace apron. Sonia wears a red dress with white scarf. Her *sarafan* has blue trim at the neck, sleeves, and hem. Olga has the most elaborate costume, with the pom-pom hat. Her costume includes a blouse, a *sarafan*, and a vest over the top that copies an eighteenth-century costume. Olga, in her peasant outfit with scarf, is the only one with a tag, which reads "MADE IN SOVIET / UNION."

Olga

Anna

Sonia

Circa 1930–1940 These dolls show more of the peasant costume variety seen in this 10-inch series of dolls. All the dolls of this type have their socks sewn onto their lower thighs and wear black shoes. They all use the same face mold and have sweet painted features. Those here are in mint condition except for some fading of the cloth. The tan waist-length jacket on the doll with the red hat is faded and used to be a light blue. Her tag shows a number, "1289." Her face is a coarser fabric than most of the dolls but is nicely painted.

The doll with the brown vest is marked "MADE IN SOVIET / UNION," as is the doll with the blue *sarafan* jumper over a blue-flowered blouse.

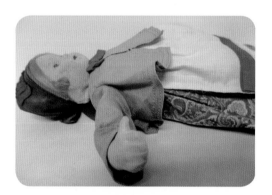

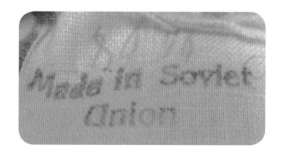

Olga

Neva

Circa 1930–1940 In many cases the outfits use the same design, with differences only in the pattern of the fabric used, as shown on these two elegant 10-inch ladies. The red flower-patterned material used for the hats and skirts on the dolls here can also be seen used on many of the other dolls in this book. This costume is one of the more frequently seen outfits representing the typical Russian peasant woman.

The tag under the skirt of the doll on the right is seen below and reads "MADE IN SOVIET / UNION."

Pictured in the 1939 *Foreign Folk Dolls* catalog produced by Kimport Dolls, the doll's name was Neva. Pictured with Neva is "Vera." She has a much-plainer peasant costume with patterned cloth apron and scarf. The cloth Kimport tag is sewn on her undergarments. Her cloth tag reads "MADE IN SOVIET UNION." Both dolls were offered for sale for $2.00 each.

#100 – 10"HIGH – $1.95 EACH

This page features the dolls called Olga and Neva from an undated Dolls of All Nations catalog page from Laura Waters Doll Studios of Washington, DC. Also offered in this catalog were tea cozies and pincushions.

Olga and Neva are pictured in the 1939 *Foreign Folk Dolls* Kimport catalog.

Circa 1930–1940 A more elegant flair is seen with these three dolls. Definitely not in peasant outfits, their clothing is elaborately detailed. Both the boy and the woman have a "bed doll" type of construction, with elongated bodies and limbs like the larger bed dolls that were popular in the 1920s. The 10-inch boy wears a Georgian-style men's coat with the same faded blue-velvet fabric as on the woman's vest. He wears a *karakul* hat with a red satin inset in the top—the same fabric as his shirt and pants. His jacket was originally a darker blue color. The jacket sports the "patron pockets" that were originally for carrying gun cartridges. Tucked into his belt is a wooden dagger.

The 11-inch lady in court costume from the fifteenth or sixteenth century has two blond braids and faux pearls on her headdress and necklace. Both have fine linen cloth on their faces, which is disintegrating. Lace runs down the front and bottom edge of her dress. The fine satin of the dress is shredding from age.

The elegantly dressed 5-inch lady has a beautiful unidentified court outfit, even though the condition of her face and hands is not good. She has leather shoes, a wonderful beaded and embroidered hat, and matching outfit. Unfortunately, the outer stockinette on her face is disintegrating and the cotton stuffing is emerging, giving her an unsettling appearance. She has no identifying tag.

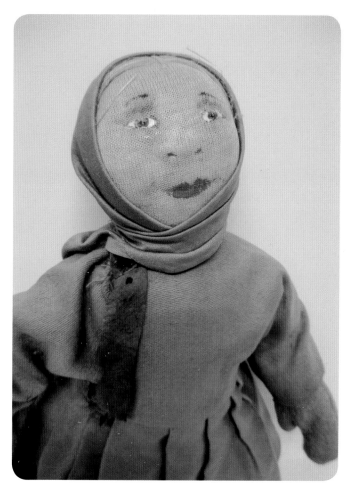

Circa 1930–1950 A stocky 12-inch-tall peasant woman is ready for the cold with her winter outfit. Though shorter, she is constructed more like the larger stockinette dolls. She wears brown felt mittens, and the left hand is on the wrong way. A long printed tag was found on her leg, underneath her clothing, which reads "Russian / Art Shop / Jewelry / Peasant Dresses / Samovar / Plaza Hotel / Asbury Park, N.J. / Everglades Club / Arcade / Palm Beach Fla."

Chapter 5
Composition

Composition is a wood or paper pulp product mixed with glue and pressed into a mold. This product came about in the late 1880s as an answer to the breakable bisque and china dolls. Many countries used it to produce dolls and other toys before plastic came into use. It was advertised as an "unbreakable" product by the doll companies in the United States. Unfortunately, the manufacturers did not know at the time that while unbreakable, the material would eventually crackle or craze. With fluctuations in temperature and humidity, the composition and oil-based paint expand and contract at different rates. Some collectors prefer not to add these dolls to their collections because of the unstable nature of the material.

Composition dolls were produced in Russia from the 1930s into the 1950s. The smaller 4-to-6-inch dolls are of very poor quality and almost always have condition issues with peeling or crackled faces.

The larger dolls seem to be of better quality and are a very heavy material. Sometimes it is indeed hard to tell if the dolls are composition, hard plastic, or painted bisque. Occasionally, as you will see here, the composition heads are used on bodies with plastic limbs. Among many of the manufacturers working in various countries during this time period, older backstock materials that were closest to hand were used whenever possible, together with new materials, so interesting combinations can surface.

OLG

ANOTHER able to fi girls from bright eyed, made under and sickle, b

GI

Circa 1930–1940 These 4-inch peasant ladies have painted heads on cloth bodies. The faces are interesting character types with side-glancing eyes. Look for small cloth tags with identifying printing on the dolls— they are sometimes found on the front or underneath the aprons. Their clothing is a simple peasant outfit consisting of long blouse, skirt, apron, and scarf. Their *lapti* shoes are usually made out of yarn. Rough flax-type hair in various colors is glued on their heads.

Most have the "MADE IN SOVIET UNION" tag that indicates they were produced after 1922.

A sidebar in a Kimport catalog from the 1940s mentions 6-inch dolls similar to these on sale because their faces suffered cracking due to climate changes.

Circa 1930–1940 The facial painting on these 4-inch peasant boys gives them a lot of character. The boy with the hat has side-glancing eyes and a smile as well as nostril holes and reddish hair. The boy with the red- and white-striped shirt has a very wide-eyed appearance with large blue eyes and stiff brown hair. A very few of the boy dolls have facial hair, such as the boy with the wonderful black beard glued to his face. Two of the three boys wear *lapti*. You can see from the close-ups the damage that happens with cracked and missing composition. Stains to the clothing are also commonly found on these dolls.

Circa 1930–1940 The 4-inch peasant ladies here have different painting styles used on their faces, with variations in the eye painting. In peasant costume, one is contrasted to a 5- and 6-inch pair of larger dolls, constructed in the same way as the smaller dolls, only harder to find in the larger size. Different yet is a 5-inch girl with the black-and-white-checkered apron. She has a rounder and larger face with a shiny finish and better-quality composition that shows no signs of crazing or chipping. She has no hands, and sticks wrapped in cloth for legs.

Circa 1930–1940 This solemn peasant girl, 8½ inches tall, has a composition flange-type head (that ends at the neck) on a cloth body. With painted features, there is no hair under her checkered scarf. Faux fur trim is sewn onto the edges of her red felt vest. Her hands are cloth, with the fingers molded together. She has black leather-type boots, a white blouse, and a patterned skirt. She is not tagged or marked.

Circa 1930–1950 These three 11-inch ladies have flange heads on cloth bodies, with composition hands and feet. They all have painted faces that are very similar to the head molds used on the plastic Expo dolls. Their costumes also use a very similar pattern to the Expo doll clothing.

The countries seen here are Russia, Lithuania, and Georgia. The girl with the decorated hat that matches her light-blue apron is from Lithuania. The costume of the Georgian girl (the dark-blue costume) is almost identical to that seen on the Expo dolls (see chapter 6). Composition dolls representing the Ukraine, Moldavia, Azerbaijan, and Turkmenistan have been seen with the same attire as the Expo dolls.

Circa 1930–1950 These 10½-inch dolls are representative of the Ukraine. Their entire bodies are made of composition, with joints at the shoulders and hips. Probably produced in the 1940s, their features are painted with closed mouths and have saran-type wigs. The girl's hair is stitched down the middle. All wear the traditional red Ukrainian boots.

Designs on the shirts and blouse are printed on. The girl wears the *kersetka* or sleeveless vest, which is fastened on the left, and a simplified version of the *plakhta* panel shirt.

The boys wear *sharovary*, the wide, baggy Ukrainian trousers made of wool fabric that are tucked into their red boots. One wears red pants, the other blue. On both, the elastic has worn out around the top—hence a "baggy" appearance. Their composition is in very good condition—there is only slight crazing on their legs along the seam lines.

This paper tag came on the Georgian girl.

"Olga" from Russia was pictured in the 1965–1966 *International Dolls around the World in Eight Pages* catalog.

Uzbekistan is most likely the area this 15-inch lady represents. She is constructed of the same heavy material as the previous two dolls and is jointed at the neck, shoulders, and hips. Her fingers are molded together. She has very deep-set black eyes that sleep. There is eye shadow on the top lids of her eyes (but no painted lashes) and a closed, painted mouth. Pearl earrings are glued on. Her wig is black synthetic hair in two braids on the sides of her head.

Peach is the color of her dress, with a red vest with gold patterns painted on. The matching hat also has the gold-painted designs and is sewn onto the top of her head. This doll was purchased by the original owner in Russia in 1992.

She is very similar to a doll pictured in the Winter 2005 issue of *Doll News Magazine*, which is identified as being produced by Ivanovo in the 1960s.

A close-up of the composition and plastic hands on these two dolls

Circa 1940–1960 Larger 13½- and 15-inch ladies such as these have very heavy heads. While I had originally thought they were ceramic, upon very close examination I discovered that they do have very slight crazing on their finish. This illustrates how confusing it can be to identify some of these dolls—and while I am putting these dolls in the composition chapter, I still feel they may be a painted ceramic. The heads have very deep-set sleep eyes. The girl in red is made entirely of composition. The girl in pink has a composition head but a very light plastic body. Both bodies are jointed at the neck, shoulders, and hips. Each has blond synthetic hair with a single braid down the back. The dresses are simply made, with blouses and *sarafans* sewn together. Buttons are used so the outfits can be removed. The original owner purchased both these dolls in Russia in 1992.

Circa 1940–1960 Another representation of Uzbekistan is shown with this 17-inch girl. Her head and face have been completely painted, giving her a hard plastic look. She has one mark on her left temple, near her eyebrow. The white blouse has black, red, and white braid trim on the sleeves and is topped by a black tunic trimmed in red rickrack and apron in red, white, and gold. She has black sleep eyes and eyebrows, and her wig has two braids. Her elaborate jewelry at her neck and waist has a silver finish but is actually very light metal or plastic material. Her label reads, in part, "Ivanovo 'Toy' Doll"—the rest is unreadable. She was produced in the 1960s.

This photo is one of two from the Library of Congress's Prints and Photographs Division. The scene is identified as Russian dolls on temporary display in Sokolnik Park, Moscow, next to the American National Exhibition. This photo was taken August 5, 1959.

This is the second photograph from the Library of Congress's Prints and Photographs Division of the Russian dolls on temporary display in Sokolnik Park, Moscow, next to the American National Exhibition in August 1959.

The close-up photograph shows a doll from Armenia on the left and a doll from Bahrain on the right. The dolls may be made of composition, or the plastic may have been painted to look like composition.

Chapter 6
Plastic: 1960s Fifteen Republics

From a series of Russian postcards published in 1967 is this card titled *Bread and Salt Welcome* in English. Pictured here are dolls representing the fifteen republics of the USSR.

The World Exposition of 1967 (Expo '67) in Montreal, Canada, was an eye-opener for a young, just-getting-started doll collector. Still in high school and with limited funds for collecting, I found that international dolls were within my price range, and no one really seemed that interested in them. Most collectors at that time sought out the antique china and bisque dolls. For our family vacation, Mom and Dad took my sister, Rosemary, and me to Montreal. While there, we were told that we could each purchase one doll from each gift shop linked to the different country pavilions that we visited. Of course, I had never seen such an assortment of ethnic dolls for sale. We visited and purchased dolls from China, Lebanon, Austria, India, and Russia, to name just a few. The variety of outfits and types of people have intrigued me ever since, and Expo '67 was instrumental in inspiring my focus on ethnic dolls and costumes.

The shop that made the biggest impression on me was the USSR (Union of Soviet Socialist Republics) gift shop. Displayed behind the counter was the huge array of boxed Russian dolls—representing the fifteen Soviet republics (at that time). We agonized over which dolls to choose and then tried to tell the cashier (who spoke very little English) which dolls we wanted.

Kirzhig

Uzbekistan

I picked a girl from Kirzhig while my sister chose one from Uzbekistan. The 10-inch dolls came tied in very sturdy shoebox-size boxes with lids and small stickers that read "MADE IN USSR." The cardboard boxes have a high acid content—dolls stored in these boxes need to have a barrier placed between the doll and the box.

The dolls had plastic heads, arms, and legs with cloth bodies. The plastic had a very different look from plastic used in American dolls and has a waxlike, almost transparent finish. They were produced with a variety of head molds—at least three that are identifiable. Paint is used for the features, and the tan flesh-colored plastic is used for the skin color. Some of the dolls look ahead, while others have their eyes painted glancing to the side. There are serious versions and ones with smiling faces. The colored plastic has an almost translucent appearance—on some of the dolls, the noses are nearly see-through. The heads have flange necks with a rim, so the head can be sewn to the body. Their arms are molded to the mid-upper arm, with fingers molded together. The legs are molded to midthigh. The cloth bodies are white or pinkish cotton, with a light stuffing. The feet have shoes

molded in relief, but those lines are not necessarily followed when the shoes or boots are painted on. The wigs are glued on mohair in a variety of colors, depending on the nationality being depicted. The costumes are sewn onto the dolls.

One of the catalogs from the 1967 Expo, *Souvenirs from the Soviet Union*, mentions "a wide choice of original and even unique souvenirs from the 15 Soviet Republics—the Russian Federation, Ukraine, Byelorussia, Moldavia, Lithuania, Lettland (Latvia), Estonia, Azerbaijan, Georgia, Armenia, Turkmenia, Tajikistan, Uzbekistan, Kirghizia and Kazakhstan." These souvenirs were on sale in twenty-six shops on the Fair grounds.

Since that time it has been my goal to find one of each of the dolls from that series—which I will identify and call "Expo dolls" as we move forward with this chapter. Other almost identical dolls, which are slightly taller at 12 inches and are all plastic instead of having cloth bodies, are also included in this section. They are found in the same type of outfits as the Expo dolls, except that they have a more elongated appearance. They have socket-type heads with longer necks that give them a somewhat stiff appearance.

Some Expo dolls and some of the later plastic dolls have 2-by-1¾-inch paper tags sewn onto the back of their costumes. These tags have a bold or capped line of text in the middle of the tag that identifies the nationality, country, region, or ethnic group the doll is representing.

The top text panel on most of the tags translates as "Moscow Fabrika Gift and Toys."

Upton Sinclair and his wife with a full set of the fifteen Soviet Republic dolls. *Photo: US National Archives*

This press photo was taken in the 1960s and shows author Upton Sinclair and his wife. Handwritten on the back it reads

> Taken in the home in ____ Monroe, California 4-3-____. There ____ the Russian dolls, beautifully clad in costumes indigenous to their _____ provences, which were sent by ____ admirers Moscow (several young ladies on the staff of OGNOPU which is very similar to our LIFE magazine).

The three boxes each hold five of the plastic Expo-type dolls, representing all fifteen of the republics.

Circa 1960–1970 This group of Armenian dolls includes a combination of the 10-inch Expo dolls and the slightly taller 12-inch all-plastic later version.

The all-plastic lady in the bright yellow, white, and blue outfit was identified as Armenian on the basis of an internet photograph of a doll identical to her that still had her original tag. She is jointed at the neck, shoulders, and hips. Her features are painted on the slightly darker-brown plastic. The skin color is not painted, so the brown color of the plastic is used for her skin color. She has painted-on white socks and blue shoes. Her dress is white with yellow-printed trim, and she wears a yellow apron with blue-printed trim. The decorations are painted onto the cloth. There are blue and orange seed beads decorating her hat.

The "Dead Shot" postcard here, part of the 1967 series, shows a boy and girl in Armenian national costume. The same men's outfits seen here are also found on dolls from Georgia (see Georgian section).

Close-up of the two Azerbaijan boys, which have never been found

Circa 1960–1970 Azerbaijan is represented with girls wearing two different outfits. The 10-inch Expo girl has a light-peach/pink outfit, while the 12-inch plastic girl has a brighter outfit with an orange waistcoat over her yellow dress. Both have beads on the sides of their heads, necklaces, and hats with veils attached to the back and each side. Painted shoes and socks finish off their outfits.

The girl pictured in the postcard wears another different-colored combination of the above outfit. 10-inch composition dolls wearing this same costume have been seen with composition heads, arms, and legs on cloth bodies.

"Holiday," also a part of the 1967 postcard series showing dolls from Azerbaijan

In the "On an Evening" postcard, two Estonian girls wear different outfits representing their country. One is knitting and the other is winding yarn.

Circa 1960–1970 The Estonian lady here is one of the 12-inch dolls. The square, thin piece of paper sewn to the back of her skirt has typed in red ink "ЭСТОНСКОИ ССР," which translates as "Estonia SSR."

The boy shown in the postcard wears a brown suit, while the boys featured here are dressed in blue. Their jackets are glued closed, and their two-colored hats are sewn onto their heads. The gold buttons on the jackets are painted on. They have the same tag as the girl.

The 1965–1966 *International Dolls around the World in Eight Pages* catalog featured three Russian dolls for sale for $17.95 each, including "Pala" in her Estonian outfit. She is the 10-inch Expo-type doll.

Circa 1960–1970 A large grouping of dolls represented Belarus, Byelorussia, or White Russia, depending on the time in history you are looking at. Included here are Expo dolls as well as the 12-inch plastic dolls. Known as Byelorussia or Belorussia from 1922 to 1991, the country chose the name Belarus upon the dissolution of the USSR in 1991.

The girls are in mint condition, with the white blouses and plaid skirts with the dark-red vests and hand bands over their blond hair.

The close-up of the boy doll shows the smiling version of this doll. The head mold is the same; only the mouth is painted open, showing teeth. It is not a special mold but certainly adds some variety to these dolls.

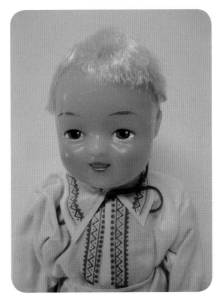

The "Mushroom Picking Party" postcard from 1967 shows a girl in Byelorussian national costume picking mushrooms.

"Anna" in her Belarus outfit as pictured in the Russian section of the 1965–1966 *International Dolls around the World in Eight Pages* catalog published by International Dolls. She was offered for sale at $17.95.

Circa 1960–1970 These Kirghiz (also spelled Kirgiz, Kyrgyz, or Kyrghyz) ladies are all the Expo dolls. The boxed doll is my original Expo girl. The material for the dresses varies in texture, but they all wear dark-green silk vests and hats with faux fur trim. Their black hair is parted in the middle and pleated in six braids in the back.

Close-ups show the faux fur hats, ribbons on the sides of the hats, and the seed beads used for necklaces. Painting varies on the faces, so even with the same head mold, the dolls look different. The braids have colored metallic thread braided into them.

One wears the typical paper tag, which has in bold lettering "КУКЛА КИРГИЗКА." It translates as "Doll Kirghiz."

The 12-inch boy wears the costume seen in the postcard, with a few variations: his belt is black instead of red, and his shoes are red instead of black. The hats are made of felted wool and are black inside and white on the outside. The tag on his outfit reads "КИРГИЗСКОЙ ССР," which translates to "Kirghiz SSR."

The Kirghiz are a Turkic people living primarily in the Kyrgyz Republic. There are also large populations living in Kyrgyzstan, Uzbekistan, China, Russia, Tajikistan, Kazakhstan, Afghanistan, and the Ukraine.

"Archery" is the title of this 1967 postcard depicting the same outfits as worn by the dolls on this page.

Circa 1960–1970 This Georgian group combines 10-inch Expo girls and 12-inch plastic boys. Georgian boys show the different colors of the men's national dress. The jackets have full skirts for ease in riding. The "patron pockets" on the front of their tunics were once used to carry gun cartridges and are now just decoration. The short dagger was part of the man's dress and highly prized heirlooms. They wear *karakuls* (hats) with a cross design in black thread on the white surface. These costumes are also shown as Armenia costumes (see the Armenian section).

This 1967 postcard titled "Dance of Lezghinka" depicts dolls in Georgian national costume.

Circa 1960–1970 These three ladies represent Kazakhstan. The doll in red is an Expo doll. All wear silk pillbox hats to match their outfits, which consist of cream-colored dresses with sleeveless belted jackets. The close-up of the back of the Kazakh Expo shows the four braids that are part of her costume.

The Kazakh boy seen in the postcard can be found in the 10- and 12-inch sizes. The boy here has a belted gray jacket over a white shirt and black pants with a printed red trim. Various faux fur material is used for the hats. His paper tag translates to "Kazakh."

This postcard is labeled (in English) "Nunters," which is probably supposed to be "Hunters." It shows a Kazakhstan boy with a falcon or hawk and his female companion.

84

The "Big Catch" shows Latvian boy and girl dolls in national costume. The girl's braids are styled differently than those of the dolls on this page.

Circa 1960–1970 Of the three Latvian girls shown here, the dolls with the white shawl draped over their shoulder are the more traditional outfits. The 12-inch girl in the checkered hat and vest is marked "LATVIA," but the outfit is seen less often.

The 12-inch boy to the right wears the outfit seen on the boy doll in the "Big Catch" postcard, with matching hat, coat, and pants. The red sash at the waist has gold-painted decorations. His *lapti* and leggings are painted on.

Circa 1960–1970 Here we have three different Lithuanian dolls—the doll in the middle is an Expo doll. The doll on the left is the same size as the Expo doll, but her head, hands, and feet are composition. The doll on the right is the taller all plastic version. The three were identified as Lithuanian from the postcard series pictures, since none of them are marked. All three are blondes with two braids hanging down their backs.

The Lithuanian boy doll pictured in the postcard has not been seen in any resource available or on the market for sale.

I also show a doll that has most likely been exposed to smoke, since she is very discolored in comparison to the other doll. Both the plastic and costume have discolored badly. Exposure to various environmental conditions can have bad consequences.

"Bon Voyage" shows a Lithuanian girl waving to a boy putting out to sea. Lithuania borders the Baltic Sea.

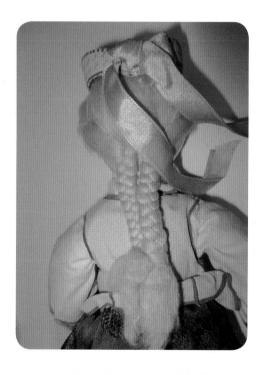

Circa 1960–1970 Traditional Moldavian costumes are showcased in these four ladies, the two in the middle being the Expo dolls. They have different facial expressions—a smiling face and a serious face (as do two of the boys). These have the same head mold, but with the lips painted to look open with teeth or closed. The open-mouth faces are harder to find. A close-up of the gold foil tag attached to the smiling boy reads the same on both sides: "MADE IN USSR."

The three Moldavian boys wear *karakul* hats and traditional outfits. Two of the three dolls have paper tags that translate as "Moldavia." Hats can be black or red. Moldavian girls in composition wearing the same traditional outfits are seen.

This 1967 postcard titled "Grapes" shows a Moldavian girl with two boys.

Circa 1960– 1970 Among the four Russian girls shown here, the dresses vary only slightly. The most common outfit includes a white blouse, colored skirt, and yellowish-with-red straps. The headdresses are decorated on the sides with white pom-poms (which would in reality be made of swan's down).

Both the Russian boys are carrying their balalaikas and are wearing red shirts, purple pants, and black boots—their musical instruments are tied to their hands and sewn to their shirts. The Expo boy has the smiling mouth seen in some of the dolls. He has curly blond hair and a very cheery expression. He wears the same outfit as the 12-inch plastic boy, only the taller boy still has his original black hat.

Circa 1960– 1970 This Russian boy, mint in box with his balalaika, was purchased at Expo '67. Inside the box was this printed paper from the Soviet Pavilion. The brochure, written both in English and French, describes some of the 4,500 different souvenirs from the fifteen Soviet republics that were available for sale. It lists many of the items available, including "dolls in national costume," as well as the clay Dymkovo figurines, *matryoshka*s, and other fine crafts.

SOVIET PAVILION
expo67

Do you know:
• that the Soviet souvenirs won 56 top awards at the World Fair in Brussels?
• that some 4500 different souvenirs from all the 15 Soviet Republics are on sale in the Soviet boutiques?
• that thousands of artist craftsmen of the Soviet Republics spared no effort and time to fully meet the requirements and taste of all visitors to EXPO-67 and that many of the souvenirs displayed in the Soviet boutiques are made specially for EXPO-67?
Welcome to our firm shops which are located in the USSR Pavilion, in Area A between the Metro station and USA Pavilion, in Area C opposite the USSR Pavilion (Upper and Lower Levels), in Area D near the French Pavilion and on the International Carrefour.

Retail Sale Centre
of the USSR Section at EXPO-67

PAVILLON SOVIÉTIQUE
expo67

saviez-vous que
• les souvenirs et mementos

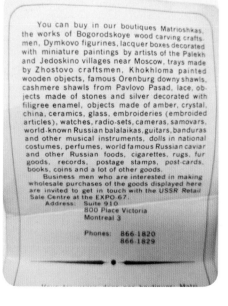

You can buy in our boutiques Matrioshkas, the works of Bogorodskoye wood carving craftsmen, Dymkovo figurines, lacquer boxes decorated with miniature paintings by artists of the Palekh and Jedoskino villages near Moscow, trays made by Zhostovo craftsmen, Khokhloma painted wooden objects, famous Orenburg downy shawls, cashmere shawls from Pavlovo Pasad, lace, objects made of stones and silver decorated with filigree enamel, objects made of amber, crystal, china, ceramics, glass, embroideries (embroidered articles), watches, radio-sets, cameras, samovars, world-known Russian balalaikas, guitars, banduras and other musical instruments, dolls in national costumes, perfumes, world famous Russian caviar and other Russian foods, cigarettes, rugs, fur goods, records, postage stamps, post-cards, books, coins and a lot of other goods.
Business men who are interested in making wholesale purchases of the goods displayed here are invited to get in touch with the USSR Retail Sale Centre at the EXPO-67.
Address: Suite 910
800 Place Victoria
Montreal 3

Phones: 866-1820
866-1829

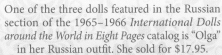

One of the three dolls featured in the Russian section of the 1965–1966 *International Dolls around the World in Eight Pages* catalog is "Olga" in her Russian outfit. She sold for $17.95.

Circa 1960–1970 Another traditional Russian girl's outfit, this time the long *sarafan* jumpers over white blouses are found here, along with the two rarely seen girls in shorter outfits. The 10-inch girl with the black-and-green vest and skirt is unmarked but probably represents Russia. The girl with the red-and-white-checkered skirt and white apron has a tag sewn inside the back of her dress that identifies her as "Russian." She has some moisture stains on her dress, apron, and hat.

There are many examples of the girls in the *sarafan*s. The paper tag from the Expo doll in the blue- and white-dotted *sarafan* reads "КУКЛА РУССКАЯ В ПЛАТОЧКЕ," which translates as "Russian doll in a head scarf."

The "In the Clearing" postcard from 1967 features a Russian boy playing an accordion for three girls in their long *sarafan*s.

A Tajik boy and girl carry a basket in the 1967 "New Crop" postcard.

Circa 1960–1970 The two boys with turbans are sometimes identified as Armenian in reference materials. However, in the postcard from the 1967 series this outfit is identified as Tajik. I use the genuine Russian reference source and consider them as representing Tajikistan.

The 10-inch Tajikistan girls come in different-colored outfits. Slight variations in painting, such as the colors and highlights of the eyes and the shape and color of the mouth, give the dolls different expressions. Notice that the bead decorations hanging down from the side of their hats are attached in different places—on the doll in the pink the beads are attached to her hat. The doll in the yellow has the beads attached to her hair, where her ears would be.

This paper tag is from the girl in yellow.

90

This round foil tag from the 10-inch boy doll has "MADE IN USSR" printed on both sides.

Circa 1960–1970 This grouping of dolls represents Turkmenistan. The two girls in the front and the boy in the middle are Expo dolls.

The boys show slight differences in stripe patterns on their robes, which cross over in the front and are belted. The boy doll in the postcard has his robe open.

The Expo boy has a round foil paper tag, with "Made in USSR" written on both sides. The hats on these boys are not as "furry" as the hat of the boy in the postcard below. A black flannel fabric circle is sewn on the crown of each hat.

A light tin decoration is sewn to the top of the hats of the girls, and four black braids can be seen hanging down under her hat. This style of girl has also been found in composition.

Postcard, like the others from 1967, called "Gift" shows a boy and girl in Turkmen costume.

The 12-inch boy has a round, blue-plastic tag hanging from his wrist. One side has a stylized design of two people who appear to be holding hands. The reverse side of the blue plastic tag has raised letters that read "MADE IN USSR."

Circa 1960–1970 A colorful combination showing color variations is seen here in these Ukrainian dolls. Colors vary for the skirts and the satin vests. Decorations on the aprons are printed on. Flowers adorn their hair as *vinok* headdresses. Some have the typical Ukrainian red boots painted on; others have painted-on white socks and red shoes. They all wear the traditional Ukrainian *kersetka* or sleeveless tunic.

The boys wear baggy *sharovary* trousers, which are traditionally made of blue wood fabric. This type of trouser is also worn by the Cossacks. The paper tag attached to the back of the Ukrainian boy doll reads "УКРАИН К А," which means "Ukraine."

"On the Outskirts" shows a boy and girl in Ukrainian national costume.

Circa 1960–1970 This grouping includes the doll purchased by my sister at Expo '67, in her box. The very splashy colored fabric used for their dresses is ikat fabric. Ikat is a dyeing technique used to pattern textiles that employs a resist dyeing process. Ikat fabric was transported through Russia on the ancient Silk Road.

The girls wear vests, the boy a red belt over his shirt and trousers. The girls have red-painted shoes; the boy has red-painted boots. The paper tag sewn onto the back of the Uzbek doll wearing the yellow-and-green dress has letters centered and bolded that read "КУКЛА УЗБЕЧКА," which translates as "Doll Uzbek."

The boys' skull caps are called *tubeteika*. This is the national headdress worn in many countries of central Asia, including Uzbekistan. The name is derived from the Turkic word *tube*, which means "top or peak." Nearly everyone wears *tubeteika*—men, women, and children. Only elderly women do not wear them.

"White Gold" shows an Uzbekistan couple harvesting cotton, which dominates the economy of their central Asian republic.

Chapter 7
Plastic: Other 1960s-1980s, to 12 Inches

A great many plastic dolls exist other than those from the series I have labeled as "Expo" dolls and the slightly taller 12-inch versions. We will take a look at them in this chapter.

An array of costumes that vary considerably in quality make up the clothing for the dolls seen here—but most often they are in historical costumes or takeoffs of historical outfits. The Ukraine is the most commonly found area when regional costumes are represented. Often, more-stylized costuming is seen than on their larger counterparts, which makes it

very difficult to identify what nationality or time period they represent.

Most of the dolls seen here are the hard plastic material like that used on the Expo dolls, with a waxlike look. In most cases, hair is glued on, eyes are usually painted on, or in some cases plastic eyes are inset. Jointing is done at the neck, shoulders, and hips.

You will see there are some mini "series" of dolls—the same type of doll available in a variety of costumes.

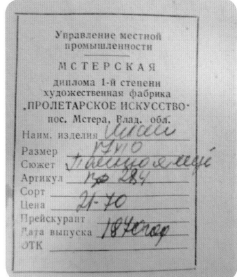

Circa 1960–1970 This miniature set consists of dolls representing the fifteen Soviet republics. They are 2½ inches tall and are hollow plastic with painted clothing and features. They are not marked. They came in a lidded box with the label pasted on the box. Sets of dolls representing the republics are also available as paper dolls and small, papier-mâché, solid cone-shaped dolls, sold as souvenirs.

Approximate identifications have been made for this set (*left to right*): Uzbekistan, Uzbekistan, Kazakhstan.

Lithuania, Moldavia, Russia

Belarus/Byelorussia, Russia, Latvia

Azerbaijan, Kirghiz, Ukraine

Georgia, unknown, Turkmenistan

Circa 1960–1970 The most commonly found souvenir dolls are these smaller plastic girls and ladies with plastic heads, hands, and feet on cloth bodies. Occasionally, all plastic versions with the same type of clothing can be found. Standing between 7 and 8 inches in height, they have more-stylized outfits than the others. Obviously there is a distinct Asian face used for the eastern areas. Several of these ladies have the blue plastic circle tag we have already seen on some of the 12-inch plastic dolls and is attributed to the Lenigruska Company. The girl with the white blouse and red- and white-striped skirt has a paper tag under her skirt that identifies her as from Byelorussia. She was purchased in the USSR in 1973.

Circa 1960–1970 These are more of the small 7½-inch dolls dressed in historically based outfits taken from the seventeenth and eighteenth centuries. As with the others, they have cloth bodies with plastic heads, arms, and legs. The same face mold is used for all of them.

The single all-plastic girl holds a loaf of bread in a sign of hospitality. Instead of painted eyes, she has plastic eyes and eyelashes. The giving of bread is a Russian tradition carried out when important, respected, or admired guests arrive at your home. The "bread and salt" comprises specially baked round bread presented with a salt shaker, usually placed on top of the bread. The bread may be on a tray or embroidered towel as this doll carries. If you are presented with this offering, you should help yourself to a piece of the bread and season it with the salt. To refuse is to greatly offend the host. Salt has been valued in Russia and many cultures since ancient times. The "bread and salt" tradition appeared in Russia before the fifteenth century.

Circa 1960–1970 Standing 8½ inches, these two young gentlemen play music for the girl who was purchased with the boy with the green hat. From the 1960s or 1970s, they are all plastic and jointed at the neck, shoulders, and hips. They have molded and painted boots and shoes. The arms on these dolls are slightly curved, with the hands cupped and the fingers molded together.

The girl with the tall hat is dressed in historical costume. She has a tag at her waist that is handwritten and reads "16th Century (class next to Tsar)." She is very similar to the others here.

Circa 1960–1970 Wearing traditional outfits, these 10-inch girls have similar construction. Both have plastic inset eyes with long, black, plastic eyelashes. Single braids hang down the back of their heads, the brunette with a fiber that is almost "woolly" in feel. While the heads of these dolls are very similar, there are slight differences in the molding of the nose and mouth. Their bodies are constructed of a very light, expensive plastic. The blonde girl is almost definitely in Ukrainian costume. She wears a white blouse with red flower embroidery and a *poneva*, the Ukrainian wraparound skirt, under her white apron. Her shoes are off-white plastic.

The *kokoshnik* on the brunette girl is made of cardboard with white, blue, and pink flowers. She has a long, white blouse or *rubakha* under her *sarafan* jumper. Her red boots are actually red stockings with black fabric glued on for the soles, covered around the edges with red trim.

98

Circa 1960–1970 Kazakhstan is the home of this 9½-inch girl with the Asian features. She is dressed in a white-and-light-mint-colored outfit with matching hat. Her face is a different mold from any of the others here. She wears black plastic shoes.

According to the original owner, she was produced in the 1970s in the city of Alma-Ata or Almaty, the largest city in Kazakhstan. Kazakhstan acquired its independence from the USSR in 1991.

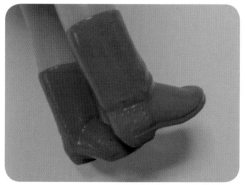

Circa 1960–1970 These Ukrainian dolls are some of the most plentiful souvenir dolls available. They have been made from the 1960s to the present time, and there is little variation in the dolls or their costumes. The pair with their box is from the 1990s, while the adjoining couple is from the 1960s. The girls wear the traditional *poneva* or wraparound skirt. The boys wear the *sharovary*, or wide, baggy Ukrainian men's trousers used by the Cossacks.

One of the labels from the end of a box has "DOLLS 'ROVENCHANKA'" written in Ukrainian.

When looking closely at the dolls, you can see that the material on the newer dolls is almost transparent in color, particularly around the nose area. All wear wigs and have painted features. Clothing is glued on.

This undated postcard, featuring a Ukrainian doll, was made for the March 8th International Woman's Day in the Ukraine. It has been a state holiday in the former Soviet Union since 1965. The Ukraine kept the holiday to celebrate the achievements of women.

Circa 1960–1970 These four boxed dolls are from Uzbekistan. All made of the harder, waxlike plastic, they are 10 inches tall. Their features are painted and they represent adults or teenagers as opposed to the younger children that are depicted on most of the dolls. The elaborate designs on the clothing are painted on. All have red molded-plastic shoes with heels, except the girl with the removable headdress. She has the same molded boots, but they are painted green. While the boxes appear to be original, they are white and light cardboard with no labels or marks, except one box has "Uzbekistan" written in pencil on the end.

Circa 1960–1970 This 10-inch doll, purchased at one of the USSR Gift Shops at Expo '67, came with her original box. She is all plastic, with painted features and a blonde wig, and is jointed at the neck, shoulders, and hips and even the waist. She wears a tan-colored, round, plastic tag that reads "Made in USSR" on one side, and a stylized picture of two figures facing each other on the other side.

The Russian letters on the box translate as "Dolls in Provincial Costume," with the company name on the reverse side. Her outfit is a historical costume, with bands of rickrack and trim used as decoration around her skirt and apron. Gold lace decorates her hat.

Circa 1960–1970 Standing 9 inches tall, this boy is all original in a very unusual rooster outfit. He is jointed at the neck, shoulders, waist, and hips with plastic curved hands. The cotton material for his outfit is yellow with black dots, and his head-dress and tail are constructed of felt.

Roosters, cocks, or cockerels (young male domestic chickens) are common characters in the world of Russian folktales. He could have been made to depict any of the following tales: *The Tale of the Golden Cockerel*; *The Fox, Hare, and Rooster*; *The Cat and the Cock*; or *The Cat and the Rooster*. Dolls of this type are typically found in festival dance costumes and are rarely seen in folktale outfits, which makes him more unusual.

Circa 1960–1970 This 10-inch pair is dressed in matching light-orange, silk-type historical or festival outfits. Both are all plastic with painted features and are jointed at the neck, shoulders, and hips. They have the same head mold and glued-on synthetic hair.

The girl has a long blonde braid that hangs down her back; the boy has his hair neatly tucked under his hat. Both have fingers molded together and turned slightly outward.

Circa 1960–1970 A variation of the last 10-inch pair is this boxed peasant couple. As opposed to the harder plastic we have become familiar with on the other dolls, this pair is made of a soft, pliable plastic. They both have rooted blond hair instead of wigs and have painted features. The end of the box translates as "Byelorussian / for children 3–8." The date on the box end is October 1979.

Circa 1960–1970 Estonia is the country represented by these 10½-inch dolls. Jointed at the neck, shoulders, and hips, they have painted features. Their light-blond wigs are glued to their heads, and their traditional clothing is glued on as well. The girls wear white blouses with striped skirts and aprons. The boy wears a white shirt, pants, and a vest. All have fabric trim headbands and wear white socks and white plastic shoes.

The paper tag on the bottom of the boxed doll dates her to 1979 and states that she is a souvenir doll.

Circa 1960–1970 These 11-inch dolls all have blond wigs, painted eyes, and black plastic glued-on eyelashes. They are jointed at the neck, shoulders, and hips. The girls all have a single long, blonde braid in the back. The boys have shorter, very light-blond hair. All have very sweet faces with a subtle smile. They wear traditional historical clothing with rickrack and braid trim. The clothing is sewn on and not removable.

This postcard is part of a series that was printed in Moscow in 1968 that features this type of plastic dolls in various poses. The postcards are all titled "Russian Souvenir."

Circa 1960–1970 These are more of the dolls from the 11-inch series seen previously. Dressed in historical costumes, they are also pictured on a series of postcards produced in Russia in the 1960s. The boy in green and the lady in pink are the same dolls as shown in the postcard. They have the same sweet faces with painted features and glued-on black plastic eyelashes that give them a very "pretty" appearance.

Circa 1960–1970 These all-plastic dolls are jointed at the neck, shoulders, and hips. The girl with the braid encircling her head has a slightly different head mold from the other dolls we have seen in this series, with a rounder shape to her head. As with the other dolls, these have wigs and sewn- or glued-on clothing. A tag found on one of the boy dolls reads "Russian Dancers 1969."

This 1968 postcard, printed in the USSR, is titled "Work Time, but Leisure Hour."

The doll in the blue dress with red stripe wears the same outfit as two of the dancing dolls on this 1968 postcard.

The girl on the postcard wears the same outfit as the doll in the previous postcard. Here a boy is bringing her a basket as a gift. Postcard printed in the USSR in 1968.

Circa 1960–1970 The Russian pair that includes the boy with the green neckerchief was purchased together, and they are most likely a couple. They are 11 inches tall and all plastic and have dark-brown wigs. They are in mint condition. They have fabric glued on their legs for stockings, as well as glued-on trim for their festival clothing.

The 11-inch pair in the red-and-white outfits was purchased as a set. The same peasant dress fabric on the girl is used for the front of the boy's shirt, and the same fabric that is used on his pants has been used for her stockings.

This dancing pair is shown on another "Russian Souvenir" postcard printed in 1968.

Representatives of Moldavia

Circa 1960–1970 Boxed 10-to-12-inch couples such as these are often found. They were produced in the 1980s and 1990s. Two face molds, one smiling and one puckering, seem to be the ones used for these dolls, with different painting to depict different ethnic groups. All are jointed at the neck, shoulders, and hips and are of hard plastic. Their hands are molded, with the palms facing out. The clothing is glued on and they have cloth shoes and wigs. They wear matching outfits, using the same fabric and trim, and can often be matched even if they do not have their original boxes.

An unidentified couple

Written on paper inside the box are the names of these two dolls: Ionas and Layma or Laine. They come from Lithuania or Latvia.

Arvice and Aet represent the country of Estonia.

These dolls are 12 inches in height, all hard plastic, and jointed at the neck, shoulders, and hips. The boys have painted hair; the girls have wigs. All have dark, large, painted-on eyebrows. The seller indicated that the dolls were purchased while he was on vacation in Russia in 1967.

This is another time when identification can get confusing. Sometimes boys like these are identified as being Armenian. A similar boy pictured in a set of Russian-produced postcards show the same boy as being from Uzbekistan.

The doll on the left has hair divided into two braids in the back. The other girls have their hair divided into six braids. All wear long veils and delicate netting for underskirts. Veils are straight in the back or bunched into two sections—one on either side of the head.

Circa 1960–1980 A printed paper was included in each of the boxed sets (printed in Russian) that translates as "Souvenir couple dolls are designed to meet the requirements of the Association of Museum of Ethnography experts and reflect national peculiarities dress." This reference to the museum is the Russian Museum of Ethnography in St. Petersburg, which has thousands of cultural items in their collection.

The couple with the boy wearing the fur hat is from Kazakhstan and have gold decorations printed onto their silk costumes. The Kazakh girl has the head mold with the lips puckered together, while the boy has the smiling face. They are dated to 1987. The set with the girl with the white-braid headdress is dated to 1993 on the box.

Dolls named Makut and Gulnat represent Kazakhstan or Uzbekistan.

This boxed pair probably represents Azerbaijan.

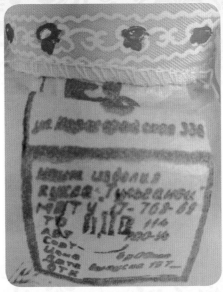

An older paper tag still remains on the girl on the far left in the group picture.

The paper tag on the boy translates as "Timurid," which is a time period in ancient Mongolia.

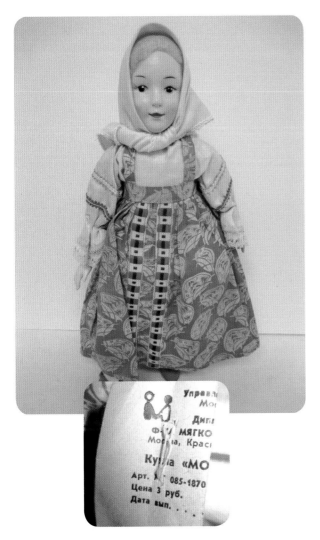

Circa 1960s–1970s The head mold on this 12-inch girl is more unusual. Her pale complexion is due to fading. You can see the brighter tan flesh color on the right side of her cheek. She has brown-painted eyes and a blonde mohair wig. Her plastic arms come up to the elbow, and her plastic legs go up to the hip, unlike the other plastic dolls. She wears the traditional *sarafan* but has real red cloth shoes instead of the molded and painted shoes. Her paper tag, which is sewn onto the back of her jumper, translates as "Doll Moscow." I have seen this head mold only one other time—on the tea cozy doll.

Chapter 8
Plastic: Other 1960s-1980s, 12 Inches and Taller

The majority of the plastic dolls larger than 12 inches are constructed of the hard-plastic material seen on the smaller dolls, but the material is a solid color and does not have the transparent or waxlike appearance seen earlier.

While the hair is still in wig form, the eyes on many of these dolls sleep instead of being painted. Jointed at the neck, shoulder, and hips, these dolls often have paper tags sewn into the lining of their undergarments. Dressed in historical clothing, the outfits sometimes have buttons so the clothes are removable.

Some of the dolls are constructed of a much-softer plastic material, very similar to the softer vinyl dolls produced in the 1960s and 1970s by companies in the United States. Probably constructed in the 1980s, these have sleep eyes and rooted hair and are jointed at the neck, shoulders, and hips—though moving their limbs is sometimes difficult because of the soft quality of the plastic. All the following dolls are jointed this way unless stated otherwise.

None of the dolls are marked in any way as to the manufacturer.

Circa 1970s–1980s All four of these 12-inch dolls use the same head mold but represent different areas. Their faces are solemn, and they have hands with the fingers together and turned with the palms to the back. All were produced in the late 1970s and early 1980s.

The boy in the black suit wears the traditional Georgian man's outfit. The boy in the white outfit has his tag tucked into his belt; the lettering translates as "Byelorussian."

The girl has a paper tag that reads "Moscow Factory Souvenirs and Gift Toys / Gift doll in the female national costume of / the Latvian SSR from the series / 'Friendship of Peoples' / 1979." The boy in green and red with the black vest and faux fur hat is not identified but could be Uzbekistan.

Circa 1970s–1980s The 14-inch soft-vinyl girl was probably produced in the 1960s. She has sleep eyes, rooted blonde hair, and pursed lips and is jointed at the neck, shoulders, and hips. Her shoes are a turquoise plastic molded to look like plastic *lapti*. They are tied on with black string. Her dress includes an unusual hat that is cloth and gathered in the middle in the back—more than a bow. She represents the Kursk region.

The 13-inch couple is constructed of the same type of soft vinyl material and dressed in yet another historical-type costume. They have the same type of face with sleep eyes and rooted hair. The boy has painted freckles and also wears the molded *lapti* shoes, only tan in color.

Circa 1970s–1980s These three 13-to-14-inch harder-plastic girls have very sweet faces with painted features. They have blonde wigs, with one long braid in the back, and painted blue eyes with painted brown eyebrows and lashes.

They wear typical peasant outfits with dresses and aprons. All wear socks and plastic slip-on shoes. The two dolls on each end have their original bags hanging over their shoulder—this is missing from the middle doll.

The paper tag sewn underneath the dress of the doll in the middle reads "Leningrad / Productions / Association / "TOY" / Doll-Souvenir / 'NASTYA.'"

Her tag translates as "Dolls—souvenir GIRL / In costume performing / In theme of folk clothing / KURSK REGION / NZ Series RUSSIA."

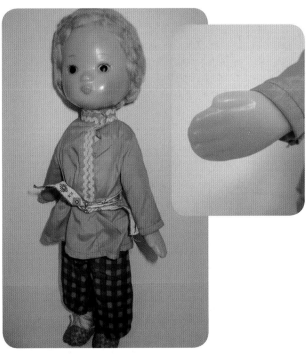

Circa 1970s–1980s This 15-inch hard-plastic girl is dressed in a blue *sarafan* with matching kerchief. She has painted features and stiff, black-plastic eyelashes. Her *lapti* shoes are also plastic and printed to look like they are woven. Her tag reads "Toy Doll Gift Masha" and is dated "Oct 1979."

The 15-inch hard-plastic boy wears a pink-colored *kosovorotka* or shirt with white rickrack decoration. He appears to have been played with, so his green-and-red-plaid pants may not be original. He has painted features and is jointed at the neck, shoulders, and hips. The photo of his hand shows that it is molded slightly cupped, with the fingers and thumbs molded together.

Circa 1970s–1980s This interesting 15-inch hard-plastic couple looks to be Ukrainian. They both have round eyes made of inset black plastic, as well as black-plastic, glued-on eyelashes. The girl has very interesting eyebrow painting. She has red lips; he has pale lips.

Both wear the traditional red Ukrainian boots. The boy wears *sharovary*, the baggy Ukrainian men's trousers. There is no tag or label on either doll.

The Ukrainian boy with the *papakha* hat is also 15 inches and has the same type of body construction as the pair. He has a paper tag tucked into his sash. The tag was stamped "1981"—probably the date for the couple as well.

Circa 1970s–1980s There are a great number of these happy Russian plastics for sale today. A Ukrainian boy is also available. They are 17½ tall and of the softer vinyl material. Be careful, since the heads do dent if the dolls are packed with things on top of them. They all have sleep eyes and smiling features with wigs and are jointed at the neck, shoulders, and hips.

These two represent the Ukraine. They wear the Ukrainian panel skirt or *plakhta* and the *kersetka* or sleeveless waistcoat. The design on their blouses is printed on but would have been embroidered on the real blouses. Both are unmarried girls with the single braid in the back.

Circa 1970s–1980s These 18-inch ladies wear a white- and blue-striped kerchief and have the wool patterned vests over their skirts and blouses. Their blue eyes sleep and they use the same head mold as the Ukrainian girls. They are of the same softer-plastic material and are quite plentiful. They have interesting shoes—which appear on all these dolls—that are leather in brown or blue, gathered around the edge and tied at the ankle.

The Ukrainian boy is the same as the girls but wears the typical Ukraine boy's outfit with white shirt and pants. The shirt has the design down the front printed on in black and red.

Circa 1970s–1980s The heavier waxlike plastic is used for the construction of this 17-inch girl. She has a surprised look on her face, with round, inset, plastic eyes under long black-plastic lashes. Under her scarf is a light-blonde wig, and she wears a colorful patterned *sarafan* and has rickrack sewn onto the sleeves of her blouse instead of printed designs. Real fabric boots make up the rest of the outfit—fabric boots are more unusual.

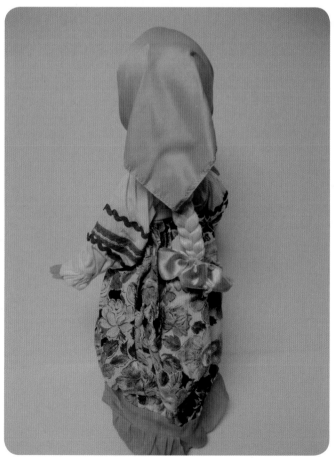

Circa 1970s–1980s This lady is 19 inches tall and dressed in an outfit from the Ukraine. She is one of many in this style that you will see here. All are hard plastic with sleep eyes. None are marked. She has brown sleep eyes and a closed mouth and is jointed at the neck, shoulders, and hips. The close-up of her hand shows how her fingers are separated.

Her close-fitting pillbox hat is called a *ochipok* and is covered with a scarf. This means that she depicts a married woman.

This handwritten tag was found pinned to the doll: "I bought this doll on my trip to Russia. Aug 1981—(Moscow)."

Circa 1970s–1980s These 19-inch ladies are more from the same series. The girl with the tall blue hat has dark-brown hair with a long braid in the back, blue sleep eyes, and a closed mouth. She is all original with no tags or marks. Her outfit depicts early Russian garb, which includes a *sarafan* over her *rubakha* or long-sleeved blouse. A doll like this one, seen for sale on the internet, was identified by the seller as Ukrainian.

The lady with the green hat has a white veil attached to the back that flows down to the ground behind her and is identified as a northern Russian outfit. She has a blonde mohair wig with a braid down the back, blue sleep eyes, and closed mouth.

The lady with the tall, pink *kokoshnik* has brown sleep eyes and wears another interesting historical outfit. Various elements of these historical outfits are combined in many different ways, so making specific identifications is very difficult.

Circa 1970s–1980s These dolls are made using the same mold as the previous dolls. The exotic with the black braid is 20 inches tall. She has a blushing complexion with blue sleep eyes and a black mohair wig with the braid in the back.

Her costume is faded badly in the front, and her headdress has only the remains of gold fringe on the bottom edge. Ribbons hang down the back of her hat.

The lady with the high hat wears the costume from the Voronezh Oblast in Russia. She has the same type of fringe around her neck of her dress that is seen on the Ukrainian doll.

Circa 1970s–1980s Two different head molds are used for these dolls from Estonia. Standing 18 and 19 inches tall, they both have sleep eyes. Their blonde mohair wigs have two braids. The cone-shaped hats are removable and often get separated from the dolls. The dolls' heads are from different molds—the face of the doll with the box has a much more "cheeky" look; the other has a very pointed chin. Both wear black plastic shoes with molded flower designs.

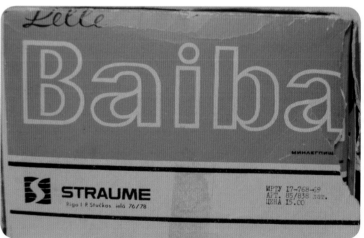

The end of the box reads "*Lelle* / *Baibe.*" The company is Straume.

Circa 1970s–1980s Estonia is represented again with these two hard-plastic ladies with a different head mold. The girl with the blue plaid skirt has lost her tall hat. The eyes of these dolls are inset plastic and have the common black-plastic eyelashes. The Estonia girl with the black skirt has lost her cape and has two braids instead of one.

With them is another doll with the same plastic molding, only dressed in a red-and-gold *sarafan* with matching hat. She has the two braids but has dark-blue sleep eyes with heavy black-plastic lashes.

Circa 1970s– 1980s The girl with the scarf is one of this series, only dressed in peasant costume. She has light-brown mohair wig, blue sleep eyes, and closed mouth. There is beaded fringe around her collar, with colored thread used to make tassels. Her kerchief is worn by village or peasant women.

The lady with the pillbox-type hat is wearing a Ryazan outfit that consists of a blouse, skirt, apron, and long vest. She has tassels on her outfit—white ones that are attached to the sides of her hat. Her dark-brown hair hangs in a braid down her back.

Circa 1981 "Welcome" is the banner carried by this soft-vinyl 21-inch lady in her fancy dress and hat. She is mint in box, and her red hair is a wig with a long braid in the back with red ribbon woven into the end of her braid. She is in historical garb and carries a white cloth with painted designs that would be embroidered on a real item.

The writing on the cloth, as well as on the paper tag above from the end of her box, translates as "Welcome." Her box lid reads "Doll."

Circa 1970s–1980s These dolls also are dressed in Estonian outfits, though different from the previous dolls seen. Also 19 inches tall, they have longer, more angularly shaped faces.

The doll in her original box has brown eyes, the other doll blue eyes. Both have blonde mohair wigs with two braids. Note the pretty silver-type brooches that the two ladies wear on their bodices, which are made of a light tin-type material.

The plaid box identifies the doll as being produced or distributed by Straume and gives the doll's name as "AYNA." One of the dolls has a tag sewn inside the seam of her skirt. The tag dates her to 1979.

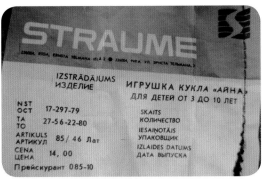

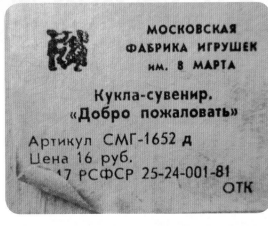

Circa 1970s–1980s More of the soft-vinyl dolls in the 19-inch size, these girls have rooted hair and sleep eyes. The girl with the red hair has pale lips and blue plastic beads as part of her outfit, which consists of a blouse, skirt, and matching vest. The decoration on her skirt, like many of the others, is printed on, not decorated with embroidery, braid, or rickrack. Her slip is a heavy fabric similar to fabric backing. Sewn into the seam of the slip you can sometimes still find the paper tag sewn along the edge. Her paper tag reads "Toy Doll MARIA for children from 5–10 years." The tag is dated 1979.

The doll with the blue-and-white scarf that covers her hat shows one of the problems commonly found with these dolls. The paint used for her lips has bled onto the surrounding plastic on her skin, which makes her look like she has chapped lips, and this cannot be corrected.

She is all original with an elaborate historical outfit complete with blue leather boots and layers of underskirts. Her tag reads "Doll-souvenir / based on Russian / FOLK CLOTHES / MOSCOW GUBERNIA." She cost 16 rubles and is dated 1969. Gubernia is a unit of local government established in the eighteenth century under Peter the Great.

Circa 1970s–1980s Both ladies here are 21 inches tall and made of the soft vinyl material. Both have wigs, one blonde and one red. The blonde girl has a cloth decoration, heart shaped and tied to the end of her single braid. The decoration on her apron is printed on. She has red cloth boots like those worn by the Ukrainians. Her tag, which is sewn up under her paper-type petticoat, translates to "Doll Sgarinnom / Folk Costume / Tamovskoi Region / A series of Russian Outfits." There is a Tambov Oblast (state or province) in Russia that it may be referring to. The other lady has no tag. She has green sleep eyes with black lashes and is all original in her historical outfit. This is one of the more common outfits.

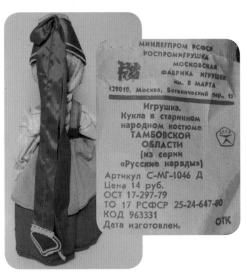

Circa 1970s–1980s Another of the soft-plastic dolls measuring 21 inches tall, including her hat. She also has the "bleeding lips" problem found often with this type of plastic. She has an interesting historical outfit. Notice that the bottom edge of her skirt has a "ream" on it, and the fabric turns up all around the edge. She has the remains of a tag that only has the date—1986—remaining.

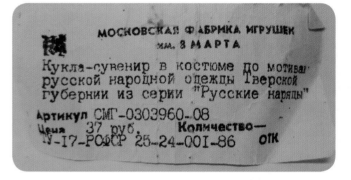

Circa 1970s–1980s Unusual is a 20-inch lady with gray hair in braids on each side of her head, thus depicting an older woman—which is rarely found. Additional decoration on her hair includes red plastic beads. Her *sarafan* jumper is a maroon color with decoration of yellow-gold silkscreen printed on the front and around the side and back. Both dolls are constructed of the soft, pliable plastic from the 1970s to 1980s.

The girl with the red hair and braid shows what water damage can do to these outfits. The fabric appears to be very inexpensive material and is easily stained, as the stains show in the sleeves of this outfit.

The tag on the doll in pink identifies her as from the Kostroma Province and dates her to 1979. Kostroma is the name of an oblast (province) and also the main city within that oblast.

Circa 1970s–1980s These two soft-vinyl ladies are 19 and 22 inches, including their large, soft-plastic *kokoshniks*. They have their fingers molded together and wigs instead of rooted hair. They wear the *rubakha* or long-sleeved blouse under their *sarafan*s or jumpers.

Vologda is a town and oblast (province) in Russia. Its lace was produced in northern Russia beginning in the seventeenth century. At the beginning of the twentieth century, this lace weaving was done by about 40,000 skilled workers. During the Soviet period, domestic lace was considered as excess, and its consumption was minimized.

The doll in red has a blonde wig and green sleep eyes. The doll in blue has a red wig with green eyes. Both have black-plastic lashes. Plastic colored "beads" decorate the *kokoshnik*.

The tag found on the doll in blue translates as "Vologda Lace." It probably refers to the lace *kokoshniks* or hats worn by ladies.

Circa 1970s–1980s Male dolls are less often seen, particularly in the larger sizes. These two peasant boys are 20 inches and constructed of the same soft vinyl that the ladies are made of, and have the same head mold. They have blue sleep eyes, rooted light-blond hair, painted-on lips, and freckles.

Their shirts have painted designs at the neck, chest, wrists, and hem. Black faux leather boots are seen under their black pants.

There is a paper tag glued into the inside of his shirt of the boy with the flowers still glued to the front of his black cap. It translates as "A toy / Doll IVAN / For children from 5 to 10."

Chapter 9
Plastic Characters, Puppets, and Miscellaneous

All cultures have characters that are linked to various folktales or stories that have been passed down through history. Russian folktales have roots that go back to the ancient Slavs. In the nineteenth century these tales began to be translated into English. Some of the early translations included *Russian Folk Tales* (1873) by William Ralston, and *Tales and Legends from the Land of the Tzar* (1890) by Edith Hodgetts. Some Russian poets, such as Alexander Pushkin, created very popular original fairy-tale poems based on traditional folktales. Illustrations by artist Ivan Bilibin make the characters come alive with their rich designs.

This chapter focuses on characters from folktales, as well as some that may not illustrate a particular person but are "character"-type dolls. This use of the term "character" is a standard classification in doll collecting, referring to dolls made with features depicting a specific facial expression (e.g., laughing, crying, wrinkled older person) or a character, as distinguished from the standard "dolly faces" used for most dolls.

Construction of the dolls varies with combinations of plastic and cloth, wire armature, and even wooden bases for some. Also included here are hand puppets, flat dolls similar to the modern "Flatsy" doll, and mechanicals.

Circa 1970s–1980s These interesting characters are some of the available souvenir-type dolls representing the Ukraine. All have hard-plastic heads and arms, with wire armature bodies, painted features, and black inset button eyes. Black mustaches are made of yarn. The dolls are mounted on pieces of natural wood, with labels sometimes found glued to their bases. Some carry jugs, others musical instruments or baskets. Even with what appears to be simple construction, their clothing has embroidered designs when we would expect to see less expensive printed-on designs instead.

One of the 8-inch men is standing next to his box so you can see how the boxes are illustrated. Most of the men carry woven cloth bags over their shoulders. One of the features is his tall *papakha* wool hat, which can be gray or black in color.

The girl pictured here is 5½ inches tall, with the same type of body construction as the men. She has yarn hair and painted features. She is missing a basket that she would have held over her shoulder. Dolls of this kind are found in abundance.

This label is glued onto the bottom of the wood platform the man with the jugs stands on. It translates as "Tulburel."

Circa 1970s–1980s With the man standing 7 inches tall, this couple seems to be having a party. Mounted on a wooden base, the Ukrainian boy is playing a plastic flute and the girl seems to be enjoying the music.

They have the same type of construction, with wire armature and plastic heads, hands, and feet or shoes, and wear traditional clothing with embroidered designs. The paper tag is glued to the bottom of their base. Individual dolls, both male and female, are usually found as well as some of these couples.

Circa 1970s–1980s The Ukraine is depicted with this unusual couple. The man is 11½ inches, the woman 10½ inches. Made of heavy plastic, they have molded and painted features and hair, have plastic hands and feet, and are on cloth bodies with wire armature. The man holds a pig wrapped in a blanket under his left arm.

The man is adorned with a molded *chupryna* or forelock, also known as a chub, which is part of a Cossack's traditional look. The long lock of hair is left uncut, with the rest of the hair shaved close to the head. It was a special sign of a Cossack nobleman and was considered dishonorable if it was cut.

Among the beliefs associated with this lock of hair is the legend that an angel sat on the right shoulder of the Cossack and guided him to do good deeds. On the left side sat a devil that was brushed off by the forelock.

He has a molded earring on his right ear, which was worn as an amulet for good luck. The woman has a pleasant face with side-glancing eyes and molded brown hair. Both are dressed in peasant costumes.

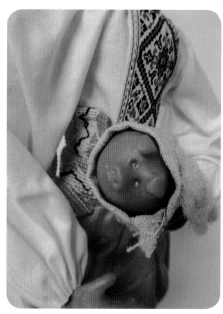

Circa 1970s–1990s The small, chubby 7-inch man on the left is known as Cossack Chub, a character from a story by Nikolai Gogol (1809–1852) titled "Evenings on a Farm near Dikanka." This story was from a collection of fairy tales based on Ukrainian folklore that were published in 1832. The story was made into an opera titled *Night before Christmas* by Nikolai Rimsky-Korsakov (1844–1908). Dolls like these were produced in the 1980s at the Moscow Toy Factory. The Russian retailers marketing this doll refer to the plastic he is made of as PVC. Chub has a painted face with a molded mustache, hands, and shoes. A popular souvenir doll, according to notes on the boxes, Chub was assembled by hand in fourteenth- to fifteenth-century Cossack-period clothing. You often find him in a silkscreened box.

What is unusual is to find all three of the characters from the story still together, tied onto their original cardboard, which was probably the backing cardboard in their original box. Here is Chub with his 8-inch wife and another unknown 8-inch man with molded and painted features, including a beard and a small ponytail also of molded plastic.

Circa 1970s–1990s Different variations of Chub's wife, all 7 to 8 inches, show the interesting combinations of material on these traditional Ukrainian outfits. All wear the *kersetka* or sleeveless waistcoat and the *poneva*, which is a wraparound skirt worn in the southern part of the Ukraine.

From the close-up of the hand construction you can see that the hands are molded flat, with all the fingers molded together except the thumb.

A lady like these was featured in a 1970s catalog produced by Dolls International, located in Kingston, Ontario, Canada. The description calls her the wife of "Chub," and he was also offered for sale but was not pictured in the catalog. Each sold for $6.95.

Circa 1970s–1990s Another delightful character is this 6-inch boy who may be one of the characters with Chub, since you sometimes see him for sale with Chub and Chub's wife. He has a character face complete with red nose and is constructed the same way. He wears the typical *kosovorotka* or man's shirt and *sharovary* (loose, baggy Ukrainian pants). His shoes and the ropes of his leggings are painted on.

He may be the folktale character Yemelya. According to the story, this young man, depicted as lazy, comes across a magic fish. The fish, like a genie, will grant Yemelya three wishes if he sets the fish free. In the end the boy makes a young princess fall in love with him, and they live happily ever after.

Another character very similar to the other dolls here is this 8-inch girl. Constructed in the exact same way, her head mold is very different, and she is much harder to find. She is shown here with Chub's wife for comparison. She has no tags.

The all-original man also has his paper tag, which translates as "Old Manager."

Circa 1970s–1990s These dolls, all 13 inches tall, represent Old Man Khottabych. Produced in the 1970s, they have plastic heads, hands, and feet with soft cloth bodies. Their genie-type shoes are molded and painted. They have delightful character faces with long, white beards. Two are missing their turbans.

Old Man Khottabych is a character from a child's book written by Lazar Lagin. In the United States the book was published under the title *The Flying Carpet*. A film based on the book was produced in the USSR in 1956.

According to the story, Volka, a 12-year-old Soviet Young Pioneer, discovered an ancient vessel at the bottom of a river. When he opens it, a genie emerges. He calls himself Hassan Abdul-rahman ibn Khattab, but Volka renames him Khottabych. The grateful genie is ready to fulfill any of Volka's wishes, but the moral of the story soon becomes evident: be careful what you wish for, because the results may be unforeseen and *not* what you wished for.

Circa 1970s–1990s A couple of interesting characters are seen here. The 10-inch boy has molded and painted blond hair and painted features with a cute smile and side-glancing eyes. His head is a soft vinyl with a flange neck attached to a softly stuffed cloth body with plastic hands and feet. He has molded and painted *lapti*.

The 9-inch Cossack man has a chubby, stuffed-cloth body with hard-plastic head, hands, and feet with painted black boots. His hair and mustache are molded and painted, similar to the Ukrainian couple seen earlier. Both dolls were probably manufactured in the 1960s or 1970s.

Circa 1980s–1990s The story of the Snow Maiden or *Snegurochka* is told in Russian fairy tales. Snegurochka is the granddaughter and helper of Grandfather Frost, also known as Old Man Frost or, in Russian, *Ded Moroz*, during the New Year. She traditionally wears long, light-blue robes and a fur hat or snowflake-decorated crown.

This 13-inch version is all hard plastic with blonde wig, inset plastic eyes and eyelashes, and a puckered mouth. Her light-blue robe has faded with exposure to sunlight on the front—you can see the brighter blue in the back-view photo. She is jointed at the neck, shoulders, and hips.

Circa 1980s–1990s Several versions of puppets have been found on the secondary market. The two character ladies are *morozko* or stick puppets. They are 9 inches tall and have plastic heads, hands, and torsos with cardboard lower bodies. These two are manipulated by movement of a single plastic rod that sticks through the bottom of the cardboard base. Both have character faces—a grumpy old woman with white hair and a sad lady with a pink kerchief.

The only hand puppets that are currently known to exist include these three characters: an old man or grandfather, an old woman or grandmother, and a girl. A teenage boy is missing from this set. The man is the tallest, standing at 18 inches tall, the old woman is 15 inches, and the girl is 13 inches. All have black-plastic inset eyes and molded and painted features with glued-on hair. They have hard-plastic flange heads and hands, and a sleeve at the bottom for your hand.

Circa 1980s–1990s Occasionally these unusual girls are found. Though featuring more-traditional "dolly" faces, these dolls have plastic cones for their bodies instead of legs. The blonde girl in the *sarafan* is 12 inches tall, with painted features and a plastic torso that is jointed at the neck. Her plastic arms are attached to this torso. The rest of her body is the plastic cone.

The smaller, 7-inch, cone-bodied girl is clothed in a Ukrainian costume. Her arms are wire, with beads for hands. She carries a plastic jug in her right hand. She has black-plastic inset eyes and glued-on black hair.

Circa 1970s–1980s These interesting flat plastic characters are reminiscent of the American Flatsy dolls from the 1960s. The largest figures are 9 inches tall, with joints at the neck, shoulders, and hips. They have black button eyes and are made of a slightly softer plastic. Two of them wear handmade outfits; the other is unclothed so you can see how they are jointed. A dressed, smaller, 6-inch Pinocchio-type figure is constructed the same way as the larger dolls.

One doll is with her original packaging, complete with directions and two swaths of fabric and buttons to make clothing. The directions, all printed in Russian, are dated October 1979 and indicate she is from the Kirgiz Republic.

One of the girl dolls has "Mockba 80" molded onto her hair.

Circa 1970s–1980s The plastic soldier playing the accordion is 14 inches tall and appears to be singing to accompany himself. He has bushy, rooted hair, painted features, and freckles. He wears a yellow plastic medal on his shirt that reads "45 Years Old." His outfit with matching hat appears to be all original. The bold print on the paper tag that is on the inside of his cape translates to his name: Vasily Terkin.

The other boy is using the same mold but wears a peasant costume. Most of these dolls that are found are missing their accordions.

Dated 1965, this postcard is from the Russian Folk Tales series printed in Moscow.

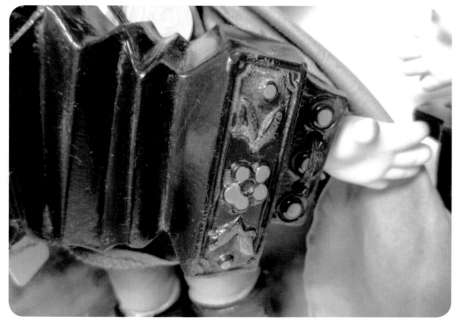

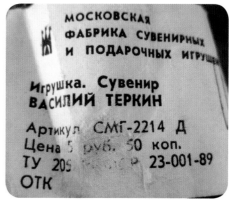

143

Circa 1970s–1980s Buffoon characters are found in various Russian folktales and also in the famous Russian circuses. This 19-inch hard-plastic boy is in mint condition and represents the traditional buffoon. He has plastic inset eyes, rooted blond hair, and a mouth with the sides painted up in clown-like fashion. He is all original, with patterned red pants, tunic with rickrack trim, and belt at the waist. His *lapti* are tan molded plastic. His clown-like hat matches the fabric on his pants. His paper tag dates him to the 1970s, reading "MARCH 8 MOSCOW." Also on the tag it reads "DOLL / THE TIMONTHY OF THE RIFT / COSTUME FASHION." International Women's Day is celebrated on March 8. Similar to our Mother's Day, this Russian holiday honors all women, including mothers, grandmothers, daughters, and girlfriends.

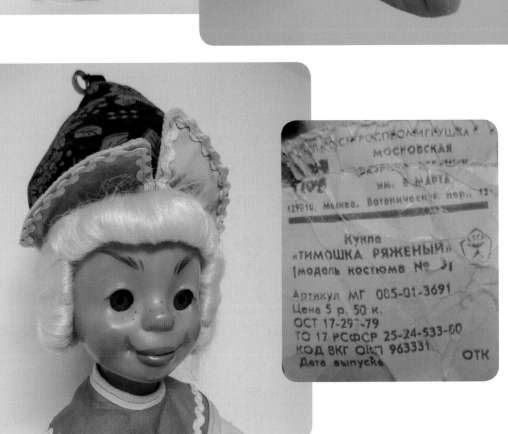

The printed cardboard box cover used for the nodding lady

Circa 1970s–1990s Small 5-inch plastic nodding dolls are often seen, all with the same mold, only with different bright colors painted on their peasant costumes. The torso and head are mounted on a plastic T-shaped base. The torso is molded in one piece, with one arm curved to the body and the other raised into the air. A bar in the torso holds the piece on the T-shaped stand. There is a grove on the inside of the head piece that holds it on the T bar and allows it to "nod."

Another commonly found doll is the *Nevalyashka* or roly-poly doll. Also a hard plastic, they come in various sizes. The torsos are round, and they usually have ball-shaped hands and heads. The large doll here is 17 inches tall, with molded and painted features and hair on a round plastic face that is inserted into the bonnet for this baby. A flower is painted on the torso—the back is plain. The smaller doll is 7 inches tall with a fancier appearance. The face and bonnet are glued together. White plastic bows have been glued to each side of the head. You can barely see the molded apron, which is not completely painted on the torso. Both have very nice musical tones that sound when the doll is moved.

Circa 1960s–1970s Much more difficult to locate are mechanical dolls. This battery-powered dancing couple has a dancing mechanism under the girl's shirt. The boy is 12 inches tall; the girl stands 10 inches tall. Both have the waxy plastic heads and arms with painted features and blond wigs. The girl is missing her hat. Other examples show the girl with a cone-shaped Estonian hat.

There is an unreadable mark on the bottom of the mechanism, and they were probably made in the 1960s or 1970s since their appearance is so much like the Expo-type dolls. Another mechanical figure that has been found is a doll pushing a doll carriage. The doll is very similar to those seen here.

Circa 1970s–1980s A character Cossack boy looking like he is ready to break into a dance, this 16-inch doll has a flat, hard-plastic head and hands with spread-out fingers. He has plastic inset eyes and a brown wig and is all original with his *papakha* wool hat and baggy *sharovary* trousers. He has fat, black plastic boots attached to his firmly stuffed cloth body. His clothing is removable. Later flat figures similar to these constructed in the 1990s have cloth heads, hands, and feet.

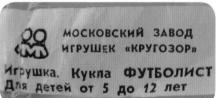

Circa 1980s–1990s A character souvenir or mascot doll related to sports is represented by this 20-inch large boy with a hard-plastic head, hands, and feet on yellow cloth body. He has a delightful face with freckles and flirty eyes that move back and forth as you move his head from side to side. His brown hair is rooted and his black boots have molded ties. He wears a yellow shirt that matches the fabric used for his body and red plaid shorts.

A cloth tag sewn inside his shirt reads "MOSCOW PLANT TOYS / Doll Football Player / 5 to 12 year olds." The original seller dated him to 1986. The pins he wears on his shirt are only souvenir items and were not original to the doll.

A smaller girl similar to this boy was manufactured, wearing a red dress made of fabric printed with teddy bears in soccer outfits. She commemorates the 1986 Ice Hockey World Championships, which took place in the Soviet Union.

Chapter 10
Tea Cozies and Pincushions

Though not technically considered dolls, the famous tea cozies and pincushions are often classified with the traditional Russian dolls and were certainly sold as souvenirs to visitors.

In the traditional way of serving tea in Russia, the top of the samovar holds a *komforka* that is made to hold a small porcelain or metal teapot or *chainik*. A tea cozy, often made in the likeness of an old woman, is used to cover the teapot and keep it warm. The *chainik* contains a very strong concentrated tea known as *zavarka*. When one wishes to have some tea, a small amount of *zavarka* is put into a tea cup, and hot water is added to taste.

The heads of the tea cozy dolls are made of a variety of materials, including stockinette, plastic, and porcelain. The porcelain dolls were probably made only as souvenirs. Some have the small cloth tags like those we have seen on the stockinette and plastic dolls in earlier chapters.

Small stockinette pincushion dolls, similar in size to the small-sized stockinette dolls, are also included in this chapter, since they have the "domestic" quality seen with the tea cozies.

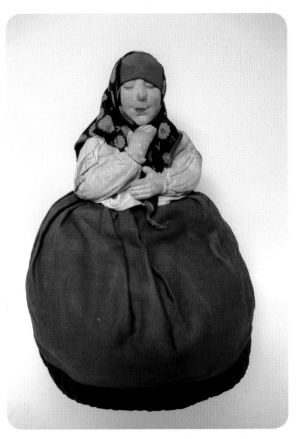

Circa 1930s–1940s Most tea cozies no longer have their cloth tags. This one is an exception. She is 12 inches in height and wears a cloth tag identifying her as a Kaluga District Woman. She has painted features with closed eyes and a serene expression on her stockinette face. Her stuffed arms are sewn to her body. She has no legs, and padding is used for her underskirt. She wears an *ochipok* or Ukrainian pillbox hat, which shows that she is a married woman.

Kimport Dolls offered tea cozies for several years in the late 1930s and 1940s through their Folk Dolls catalogs.

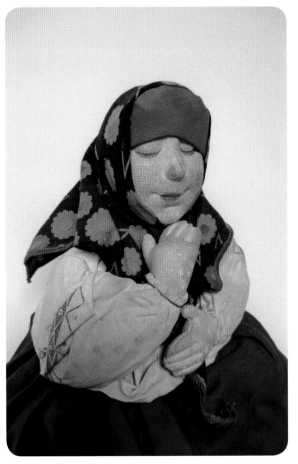

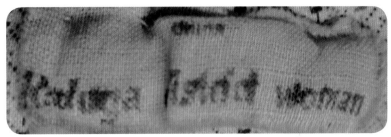

RUSSIAN COZIES

NINOTCHKA and the Gypsy are the largest, most impressive size of cozy type that were made. The heads are 4 inches high, 12 inches in circumference; Ninotchka's high waisted apron full 18 inches long. Her Slavic face is really lovely with laughing blue eyes that fairly twinkle, and lips deep wreathed with smiles. Her complexion is fair; crowned head-dress typically Russian under an extra gay babushka and the silken hands, not shown in the sketch, with folded arms are nicely proportioned and shapely.

The Gypsy also flashes a dimpled smile; her brown eyes have a life like look, and she's bedecked with beads and ear bobs falling from beneath her scarlet scarf and gilt entwined black braids.

No. 902K—Ninotchka $9.95
No. 902G—The Gypsy 9.95

MATRESHKA DOLLS OF RUSSIA

RUSSIAN nests are perhaps the

This ad is from the February 1944 *Foreign Folk Dolls* catalog produced by Kimport Dolls. It features Ninotchka and a Gypsy, both tea cozies selling for $9.95 each.

Circa 1930s–1940s This large, 15-inch lady has a fine stockinette head with painted features. Her blonde hair is a good quality of flax, and she has a very serene appearance. Her red apron covers a large skirt of printed flower material. There are red fabric inserts in the sleeves at the top of her shoulders.

The quilted padding used underneath these dolls is very thick and can make them difficult to display because of the space that is required to accommodate their dress.

Circa 1940s–1950s Environments such as smoke-filled and greasy kitchens can take their toll on artifacts; in particular, cloth articles. Standing 10 inches tall and having a skirt diameter of 12 inches, this lovely lady has suffered the adverse effects of a less-than-perfect environment, as evidenced by her yellowed and stained surface. She has flax hair and painted features and sports a tag that you can faintly read: "Made in Russ——."

Circa 1940s–1950s The stockinette material used on the dolls can vary in quality. This 10-inch doll has a very fine-quality silk-type fabric for her painted face. She has a fancier outfit than most of the cozies, which usually represent peasant women. The gold edging on her costume sets her apart from the others. The tag on her back identifies her as "GIRL IN SARAFAN."

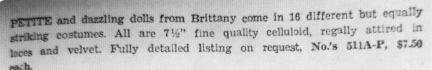

PETITE and dazzling dolls from Brittany come in 16 different but equally striking costumes. All are 7½" fine quality celluloid, regally attired in laces and velvet. Fully detailed listing on request, No.'s 511A-P, $7.50 each.

EVEN THOUGH Russian items are well nigh impossible to obtain in this era of armed camps, Kimport was lucky enough to find a small supply of tea pot covers. These are somewhat larger at 13" than our previous stock but are the same pretty young peasant girls, wearing gay headscarves and cotton blouse and skirt. Made in Russia years ago and stored away in an American warehouse 'til now, they are No. 902, price $4.95.

The 1963–1964 Kimport Dolls catalog has only one item representing Russia for sale, this 13-inch tea cozy. The description includes "Made in Russia years ago and stored away in an American warehouse 'til now . . ." The dolls sold for $4.95 each.

Circa 1960s–1980s Cozies can have plastic heads, most produced in the 1960s to the early 1980s. The 9-inch girl with the green scarf is constructed of heavy plastic. She has a plastic flange head and plastic arms that go up to the shoulder. Her body is cloth, and there is pink padding under her red dress. Gold trim and white rickrack decorate the front of her *sarafan*.

The other cozy has a soft-vinyl head with rooted brown hair and stands 13 inches tall. She has vinyl arms and torso on a cloth tea cozy base. She is jointed at the neck and shoulders. She has painted features with an open/closed mouth and sports cute freckles.

24. RUSSIA 8"
The "Tea-cosy" doll is almost wax like in appearance. Her braid trimmed dress is colourful and it has long full sleeves. She wears a white scarf around her head. A male doll is available to go with this doll.

This ad from a 1960s International Dolls catalog shows a very similar doll to the one seen here with the plastic head and hands.

Circa 1960s–1970s Larger cozies, such as these 20-inch ladies, have plastic heads with flange heads (their necks end with a groove for sewing them onto the body). They both have plastic hands and painted features. Fine synthetic blonde wigs show from under their headdresses. The small plastic hands are sewn to the torso. And, as usual, they have the stuffing underneath with no legs or feet. Both were probably produced in the 1960s.

"Scene at the Well" is the title of this 1968 postcard printed in the USSR.

Circa 1970s–1980s This is a very large tea cozy at 22 inches, and its comical face is complete with arched eyebrows and side-glancing eyes. She has a fine stockinette face with painted features. You can even see molded dimples in her chin. Her right arm is sewn to her body, while her left arm is straight at her side. Her light-blonde, almost white hair is carefully braided around her head.

Circa 1970s–1990s The Bread and Salt welcome (see chapter 7) is seen with this large 19-inch lady in her best dress. She holds a yellow cloth with a red-printed design on the ends. In the middle is a plastic round loaf of bread with a small jar of salt molded and painted on top. She holds these in her cloth hands. She has an interesting character face, similar to the doll seen earlier blowing on her tea cup.

The typical square paper tag sewn onto the back of her outfit reads "Bread and Salt."

Circa 1970s–1990s The smiling older woman is again seen with this 19-inch cozy. Her white blouse is covered with a long vest that has cloth-covered buttons sewn down the front. She carries a piece of cloth in her right hand, which is sewn to her torso.

Circa 1970s–1980s Another cheerful example in this category offers an infectious smile. Standing 20 inches, she has a molded silk face with large nose, full cheeks, and painted cheerful features. She is very fancy and wears a red plastic bead necklace and red hoop earrings. Her arms are sewn to the side of her body, and her flowered outfit is trimmed with red fabric accents.

RUSSIAN TEA-COZY

THIS tea-cozy must have well earned her name of "Gossip" for she seems to listen with hand to ear. Her full skirt with padded underskirt is just the right size to fit over the evening teapot or to conceal pajamas on the bed. Her companion, the "Tea-Soaker," (not pictured) seems to have no interest in anything save her tea. Her plump countenance rounds out in dimples and double chins.

902X—Tea-Soaker, 20" $6.00
903X—The Gossip, 20"   6.00

A smaller cozy is the pleasant, placid Farmer's Wife, typically dressed in white blouse, bright scarf and voluminous skirt.

Pictured both in the 1940 and 1941 Kimport catalogs are several tea cozies, including a "Gossip" and a "Tea-soaker" (not pictured). Each was 20 inches tall and sold for $6.00 each. A smaller 12-inch cozy representing a farmer's wife was also offered (but not pictured) for $2.50 each.

The "Tea Party" featured two tea cozies with a table, cups, and teapot in this 1968 postcard from the USSR.

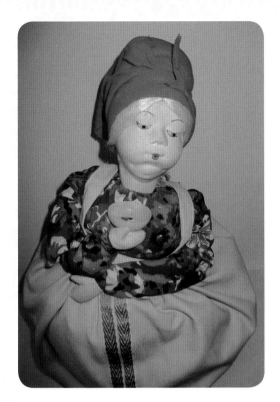

THE TEA SOAKER

THIS over sized and heavily padded tea cozy was made in Russia before their export bans against cottons and wools. We have a limited supply of this adorable old village woman who, the story goes, visits from house to house carrying her own bowl but imbibing the neighbors' tea and gossip!

She is 20" tall, but sits lower. She has carrot red hair, a ruffled print dress, stenciled shoulder shawl, silk stockinet hands and face, humorously modeled and naturally colored. Her plump countenance rounds out in dimples and double chins as she concentrates on gently blowing into her hand painted wooden bowl.

Made in the Hinterland of Russia

No. 902—Tea Soaker, 20" $5.00

Another 1941 Kimport catalog showed a photograph of the "tea soaker" lady with carrot-red hair and a facial expression of blowing on the bowl she is holding. She sold for $5.00 each.

Circa 1970s–1990s The 18-inch girl here has the same facial expression as the doll called the "tea soaker" in the Kimport ad, with her face puckered up to give the impression that she is blowing on the bowl to cool it or that she is getting ready to take a sip of her drink.

The doll with the white apron with the stripe at the bottom is marked "GOSSIP GIRL." Standing 18 inches tall, she has a red cotton scarf and orange plastic earrings. She is dated to 1969.

Circa 1980s–1990s Tea cozies with porcelain heads are less common. The girl with the short green vest is 15 inches and has a matte-finished (not shiny) porcelain head and hands. Her fancy outfit is decorated with rickrack and sewn-on braid. There is no mark.

The other doll, 2 inches taller at 17 inches, is similar to the newer porcelain dolls seen in the chapter on modern porcelain. She has a glazed china head with fired-on features and an elaborate costume decorated with braid and embroidery. Her elaborate hat is glued to her head. Her skirt is much narrower than the other tea cozies, and perhaps she is not a cozy at all but may just have been made to look like one. Since there is no tag, we do not know for sure.

Circa 1940s This diminutive 3-inch lady has a flat pincushion-type body, and fine silk on her face with painted features. She even has large, circular areas of reddish-orange blush on her cheeks.

Her simple peasant outfit has a blue silk kerchief in plain blue fabric, a polka-dot blouse, and a flowered skirt that is also her base. Her hands are the spoon-type stuffed hands with wire arms that can bend, the same type of treatment as found on the small stockinette dolls. Her body is flat and firm on the bottom, so she sits very well.

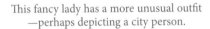
This fancy lady has a more unusual outfit
—perhaps depicting a city person.

Circa 1930s–1940s You can often find these pincushion-type dolls, both male and female. With no legs, the skirts or pants of the dolls are hard-stuffed "cushions." Most of them have fine silk-type faces with painted features. They are less often found with composition-type faces. Their bases are round and they do not stand up on their own.

Averaging 4 inches tall, they vary in costume. The two girls pictured together have long, dark hair with a single braid hanging down the back, and round, stuffed hands sewn into the empty blouse sleeves, and both wear aprons. The doll on the left has a ribbon headband with colored pom-pom decorations on the sides.

The doll with the white hair has a sticker tag on the bottom that reads "MADE IN SOVIET UNION."

The lady with the two black curls or braids on each side of her head has no hands, just gathered fabric under her shawl. She has a faded paper tag glued underneath with "1938" hand-written in ink. The lady in the brown, two-toned outfit is more unusual and probably depicts a city person.

Circa 1930s–1940s The two 4-inch tall men are dressed as Cossacks with their puffy pincushion trousers. Their comical expressions include large mustaches and furrowed brows. They both have tags on the bottom that read "MADE IN SOVIET / UNION."

Another Russian lady pincushion, 4¾ inches tall, is seen here. She has a very nicely painted face. She has the same pom-pom-style headdress as seen on some of the other pincushion type dolls, and is one of the more commonly found styles.

Chapter 11
Printed Reference Materials

The Russian plastic maiden dressed in a winter outfit with gold *kokoshnik* is wishing you a "Happy New Year!" in this 1971 postcard printed in Moscow.

Single postcards and series of postcards printed in Russia are a wonderful source of information to help identify or date Russian dolls, even if the tidbits of information are small. Some of these series of cards are included in chapters that pertain directly to certain dolls.

"New Year Gift" is the title of this 1968 postcard printed in Moscow. The dolls appear to have plastic character heads on cone bodies with cloth arms.

An all-plastic girl is being "Caught" in this 1968 postcard printed in Moscow by a stuffed terrier-type dog toy.

"Russian Dance" is the title of this Moscow postcard dated 1968.

From the same series, this postcard, also from 1968, is titled "Declaration of Love." The plastic dolls are the same type as in the "Russian Dance" postcard.

This postcard is from an undated series titled Dolls in Folk Costume. These dolls appear to be composition dolls in folk dress. This pair is from the Kostroma region.

From the same series, this doll represents the Arkhangelsk region.

Another of this series, this couple is from the Yaroslavl Oblast.

The Voronezh Oblast is seen with this couple.

The regions of Tambov and Kursk are
represented on this postcard.

The regions of Tula and Tambov are seen on this postcard.

Another couple representing the Voronezh Oblast.

This couple, also part of the Dolls in Folk Costume series, depicts the Ryazan District.

The girl at the fence in the last postcard in her Ryazan outfit is shown here with a girl from the Voronezh region.

A slightly different Ryazan outfit is seen on this girl with a boy also in Ryazan clothing.

Another girl in another variation of the Ryazan costume

This postcard printed in Moscow in 1965 shows a character-type composition girl and is titled "Doll in a Suit of Old Moscow."

This composition character boy holds up two strings of bagels and probably has more in his basket. The title of this postcard, also part of the 1965 series, is "The Boy with the Steering Wheel."

"Dance" is the title of this postcard featuring dolls from Moscow and the Kursk Oblast.

The oblasts of Ryazan (on the left) and Kursk (on the right) are seen here. The Ryazan girl wears the same dress with the traditional plaid skirt, only with a different headdress.

Titled "Uzbek Dolls," the following postcard series
consists of a complete set of sixteen cards produced by
the Red Banner Printing House in Uzbekistan in 1976.

This is the card stock cover for the following series of cards. The descriptions for the postcards are printed in six languages, including English.

The back of the cardboard sleeve

The postcard caption reads "Ceremonial Woman Dress, Margilan (left) and Andishan."

The postcard caption reads "Ceremonial Woman Dress, Khorezm (left) and Andijan."

The postcard caption reads "Ceremonial Woman Dress, Andijan."

The postcard caption reads "Ceremonial Woman Dress, Khorezm."

The postcard caption reads "Ceremonial Woman Dress, Khorezm."

The postcard caption reads "Ceremonial Woman Dress, Fergana."

The postcard caption reads "Ceremonial Male Dress, Khorezm."

The postcard caption reads "Ceremonial Male Dress, Khorezm."

The postcard caption reads "Ceremonial Woman Dress, Bukhara."

The postcard caption reads "Ceremonial Male Dress, Margilan."

The postcard caption reads "Ceremonial Male Dress, Margilan."

The postcard caption reads "Ceremonial Woman Dress, Margilan."

The postcard caption reads "Ceremonial Woman Dress, Karakalpakta."

The postcard caption reads "Ceremonial Woman Dress, Kokand."

The postcard caption reads "Ceremonial Woman Dress, Khorezm."

The postcard caption reads "Souvenir Doll in stylized folk dress."

Interesting source material can sometimes be found in old press photos. Newspaper companies over the past few years have been disposing of their old photo archives, which has sometimes led to some being made accessible to the public. These photographs are a great chronicle of history. From the 1920s into the 1950s and 1960s, there were numerous articles about young collectors who were given or collected international dolls.

Here is one young collector with her large folk doll collection. The photo has no credit line or date but was probably taken in the 1940s. She wears a Polish outfit. The entire first two rows of her collection are Russian dolls—both the smaller stockinette dolls and the smaller composition dolls.

In a photo dated ca. 1940 is this young lady with her international doll collection.

The two small stockinette dolls (Samoyed and Velikovessun) are seen on the front of the table with a couple of the small composition dolls.

Also on the table is this Kirgiz boy (on the left) with one of the dolls tagged Mascha from the chapter on small stockinettes, along with three more of the small composition dolls.

This 14-inch Eskimo woman stands in the lower middle section of the photograph.

One of the ladies from Nizhny Novgorod can be seen in the upper left side of the grouping.

In another undated photograph probably also from the 1940s, seven children are posed with dolls in folk costume. A display case, perhaps either at a school or library, has more folk dolls on the shelves, and the back of the case reads "Christmas Everywhere Foreign Dolls."

This close-up shows a Mordwa lady propped on a shelf next to a tea cozy.

Dated January 2, 1936, this press photo's caption reads:

PRESIDENT'S MOTHER SEES "DOLLS OF THE WORLD" Mrs. James Roosevelt (*left*), Mother of President Roosevelt, and some of the children of the Henry Street Settlement in New York City, look over "Dolls of the World" on exhibit at the B. Altman Department Store, which is being held for the benefit of the visiting nurses service of the Settlement, January 2.

The Henry Street Settlement, a social service organization located on Manhattan's Lower East Side and still in existence, was founded in 1893 by social worker and public-health pioneer Lillian Wald.

Photograph is credited to "Acme."

A Yakut lady stands on the right on the top shelf, next to a wooden deer.

"Detroiters Have Come from Many Lands" is the sign above the dolls featured in this press photo dated April 26, 1951. The two girls, Irene Rubin and Helen Howell, are seen looking at a variety of dolls in folk costume.

The photo credits include *Detroit News* Staff Photographer Herrmann, reporter, and finished by Warner.

A pair of large stockinette dolls consisting of a Village boy and Mordwa woman are nestled between some of the German bisque dolls dressed in foreign costume.

Dated March 20, 1962, this press photo caption reads:

Russian tot fondly pats doll her mama is considering purchasing.
Toys, games and nearly anything for children are inexpensive at
G. U. M. Dolls in provincial dress have universal appeal.

G.U.M. is a Russian abbreviation for the state-run department
store in Russia. Its branches are main department stores in many
Russian cities. There is no credit line for this photo.
The little girl is looking at a doll that is most likely plastic
with inset plastic eyes, dressed in peasant costume.

Glossary of Clothing Terms

Words and definitions used in this glossary refer to general Russian terminology unless noted to a specific cultural area or region. General references about clothing and the term "peasant" or "village" are used for the general Russian population unless a specific culture is being noted.

Armiak

armiak: A heavy cloth coat worn mainly by men. It was robe-
like and single-breasted, with straight sleeves and a large
collar. From the eighteenth to early twentieth centuries it
was worn mainly by peasants.

Kerchief

Kersetka

kerchief: Scarf worn by village or peasant women

kersetka: A Ukrainian sleeveless waistcoat or vest that is fastened on the left and decorated with cloth trims

Kokoshnik

Kosovorotka

kokoshnik: A roundish shield worn on the head, with a crest shape rising above the forehead. Although its date of origin is unknown, it is widely mentioned in folktales. It was at first worn exclusively at festivals and could be worn by married or unmarried women.

kosovorotka: A man's shirt with the buttons offset at the collar. The traditional shirt is long sleeved and reaches down to midthigh. There are buttons at the collar but not buttons all the way down. It is worn loosely and not tucked into trousers but belted with a belt or ropelike tie.

Lapti and Omacha

lapti: Shoes typically worn by peasants, woven of bast from the bark of the linden or birch tree. The wood from this same tree is used to make the matryoshka or nesting dolls famous in Russia.

Ochipok

Papakha

ochipok: A Ukrainian close-fitting pillbox hat. It is plain for everyday wear and finely embroidered for special occasions. It is covered with a scarf and is the symbol of a married woman.

onucha: The cloth strip wrapped around the leg and feet before the *lapti* are put on. They are fastened to the leg with a bast lace and twined around the shin in the manner of the old Greek sandal.

papakha: A traditional woolen hat worn by people throughout the Caucasus, including Georgians and Chechens. The hat was adopted by the Russian military, first by the Cossack cavalry and then by the czar's cavalry in the middle nineteenth century. In 1917 it was dropped from the uniform but was readopted in 1935, and in 1941 it was reserved exclusively for generals and marshals, thus symbolizing a high rank.

plakhta: A Ukrainian panel skirt woven in a square pattern.

Poneva

Rubakha

poneva: A wraparound skirt worn in the southern part of Russia, made of three straight, lengthwise strips of wool or linen. It was often made with a checkered pattern and decorated with ribbons and embroidery. It could open at the front or on the side or have no openings at all.

rubakha: A long-sleeved blouse, worn throughout Russia, that usually reaches to midthigh or full length. It usually has full- or three-quarter-length sleeves. The embroidery along the neckline, sleeves, cuffs, and hem was believed to protect the wearer from evil. The most common color is white or red. This same term can be used for the blouses both of men and women.

Sarafan

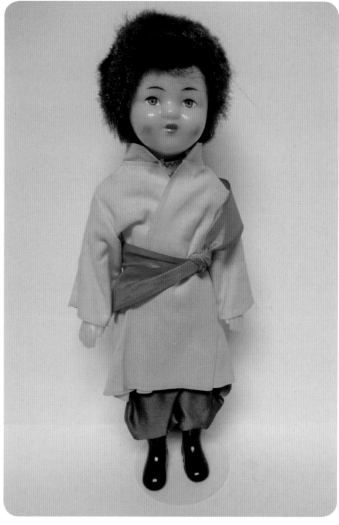

Sharovary

sarafan: A sleeveless frock or light jumper found in many areas of Russia. It can be loose fitting or fitted at the waist. Prior to the Russian Revolution, it was made of red fabric, a symbol for "beauty or beautiful." Red-colored fabrics were used for all celebration costumes.

sharovary: Wide, baggy Ukrainian men's trousers made of blue wood fabric that is tucked into boots (traditionally red). The trousers are made for ease in riding and are also worn by the Cossacks.

Suyta

suyta: A Ukrainian coat with the right side wider than the left side
in order to make a wedge-shaped overlap

Russian Terms

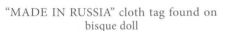

"MADE IN RUSSIA" cloth tag found on bisque doll

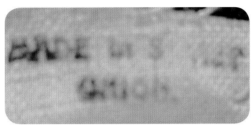

"MADE IN SOVIET UNION" cloth tag found on bisque doll

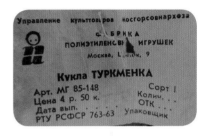

Square paper tag sewn with thread onto the skirt of an Expo doll, which identifies her as representing Kirghiz

Common words written in Russian are translated here. These words are often found on the paper tags attached to the dolls, in particular the plastic dolls.

Armenian = АРМЯНКА or АРМЯНСКОИ
Azerbazan = АЗЕРБАИДЖАНКА
Byelorussia = БЕЛОРУССКА or БЕЛОРУССА
Doll = КУКЛАl
Estonian = ЭСТОНКА or ЭСТ ОНСК ОИ ССР
Georgia = ГРУЗИНКА
Kazakh = КАЗАШКА
Kirghizka = КИРГИЗКА
Doll Kirghiz = КУКЛА КИРГИЗКА
Kirghiz SSR = КИРГИЗСКОЙ ССР
Latvian = ЛАТВИЙКА, ЛАТВИЙСКОЙ ССР
Lithuania = ЛИТОВКА
Moldavian = МОЛДАВАНКА or МОЛДАВСКО
Moscow Gubernia (Russian Empire) = МОСКОВСКОЙ ГУЬЕРНИИ
Russia or Russian = РУССКАЯ
Russian doll in a head scarf = КУКЛА РУССКАЯ В ПЛАТОЧКЕ
Tajik = ТАДЖИЧКА
Turkmen = ТУРКМЕНКА
Ukraine = УКРАИНКА or УКРАИН К А
Uzbek = УЗБЕЧКА
Doll Uzbek = КУКЛА УЗБЕЧКА

Bibliography

Cole, Adeline P. *Notes on the Collection of Dolls and Figurines at the Wenham Museum, Claflin-Richards House, Wenham, Massachusetts*. Wenham, MA: Wenham Historical Association, 1951.

Coleman, Dorothy, Elizabeth Coleman, and Evelyn Coleman. *The Collector's Encyclopedia of Dolls*. New York: Crown, 1968.

Fainges, Marjory. *The Encyclopedia of Regional Dolls*. Kenthurst, NSW, Australia: Kangaroo Press, 1994.

Frame, Linda Jean. *Folk and Foreign Costume Dolls*. Paducah, KY: Collector Books, 1980.

From the Collection of the Zagorsk Museum of Toys. Moscow: USSR Academy of Pedagogical Sciences, 1987.

Gordon, Lesley. *A Pageant of Dolls*. New York: A. A. Wyn, 1949.

Hadfield, Penny. "Russian Dolls." *Antique Doll Collector Magazine* 15, no. 6 (July 2012).

Hedrick, Susan, and Vilma Matchette. *World Colors*. New York: Hobby House, 1997.

Holz, Loretta. *The How-To Book of International Dolls*. New York: Crown, 1980.

Judd, Polly, and Pam Judd. *European Costumed Dolls Identification and Price Guide*. New York: Hobby House, 1994.

Kimport Dolls. *Foreign Folk Dolls*. Independence, MO: Kimport Dolls, 1939, 1941, 1944.

Lisiana, Elena. "Dolls of the Former Soviet Union." In *Dolls at 2000: A Celebration of Dolls at the Millennium*. Edited by Rosalie Whyel, 63–69. Kansas City, MO: United Federation of Doll Clubs, 2000.

Mingei International Museum of World Folk Art. *Folk Art of the Soviet Union: Reflections of a Rich Cultural Diversity of the Fifteen Republics*. San Diego, CA: Mingei International Museum of World Folk Art, 1989.

Russian Toys / РУССКАЯ ИГРУШКА: Album of the Art and Pedagogical Museum of Toys in Sergiev Posad. Moscow: Three Square, 2016.

Shpikalov, A. *Russian Toys*. Moscow: Progress, 1974.

Solovieva, Larissa. *Russian Souvenir: The Toy*. Moscow: Interbook Business, 2002.

Index

Akoulina, 58
Alexei, 58
Anna, 59, 81
Armenia, 43, 73, 75, 78, 83, 90, 108, 189
Attendant, 33
Azerbaijan, 68, 75, 79, 95, 108, 189
Belarus, 31, 53, 81, 95
Belorussia/Byelorussia, 53, 75, 81, 95, 96, 102, 111, 189
Chub, 134–136
Cockerel, 101
Cocks, 101
Cossack, 43, 133–134, 138, 147, 161, 185
Eskimo, 31–34, 177
Estonia, 75, 80, 103, 107, 120–121, 123, 189
Expo '67, 74, 75, 76, 88, 93, 100
Georgia, 43, 62, 68, 69, 75, 78, 83, 95, 111, 185, 189
Gogol, Nikolai, 134
Gubernia, 124, 189
Gypsy, 14, 52
Kaluga District, 149
Kazakhstan, 75, 82, 84, 95, 108, 114, 189
Kimport, 39, 57, 59, 65, 156–157
Kimport Dolls, 31, 39, 46, 47, 57, 59, 61, 149, 151
Kirgiz (Kirghiz), 51, 75, 82, 95, 112, 142, 176, 189
Kostroma, 127, 164
Kursk Region, 31, 112, 113, 165, 168
Latvia, 75, 85, 95, 107, 111, 115, 189
Lithuania, 68, 75, 86, 95, 107, 189
Man on the Road, 52
Marseille, Armand, 9
Mascha, 53, 176
Moldavia, 68, 75, 87, 95, 107, 189
Mordwa, 12, 31, 34–36, 47, 178, 180
Neva, 61

Nizhny Novgorod, 30, 36, 177
Old Man Khottabych, 137
Olga, 59, 69
Oroch, 32, 37
Roosters, 101
Russia, 7, 68, 70, 82, 88, 89, 95, 186, 189
Ryazan District, 10, 30, 31, 38, 40, 56, 122, 166–168
Samoyed, 31, 33, 49, 176
Sky Girl, 49
Smolenski, 17, 30, 31, 39
Snow Maiden, 139
Sonia, 59
Tajikistan, 50, 75, 82, 90, 189
Tambov Oblast, 125, 165
Tamovskoi Region, 125
Tanika, 58
Turkmenistan, 68, 75, 91, 95, 189
Ukraine, 20, 23, 30–32, 41, 44, 68, 75, 82, 92, 94–95, 98–99, 114–115, 117–118, 125, 131–133, 135–136, 141, 183, 185, 187–189
Uzbekistan, 51, 69, 71, 75, 82, 93, 95, 100, 108, 111, 169–174, 189
Vanika, 58
Velikovessun, 48, 176
Vera, 61
Village Boy, 31–32, 41, 180
Vologda, 128
Voronezh Province, 20, 31, 119, 165–166
White Russia, 81
Willage Boy, 31, 41
World Exposition of 1967, 74–75
Yakut Woman, 42, 179
Yemelya, 136
Ziormra, 50
Ziqanka, 14, 52

About the Author

Linda Holderbaum began collecting dolls in the 1960s, leaning toward ethnics, because they were affordable for a young collector. Over the years the collecting expanded into clothing and accessories as well. She began writing for various doll magazines in the 1970s. She was a judge for two doll exhibitions/competitions in Michigan for over 15 years and was the chairperson of the UFDC Region 12 Conference in Battle Creek in 1989. Professionally she has worked in the museum field for 30+ years as a curator and an executive director. Many of the exhibitions she curates are cultural in nature and work closely with several ethnic groups in her community. She believes that dolls are truly a mirror of man and have much to teach us.